AMERICA AT CENTURY'S END

James Schlesinger

★

AMERICA

AT

CENTURY'S

END

★

COLUMBIA UNIVERSITY PRESS
NEW YORK

COLUMBIA UNIVERSITY PRESS
NEW YORK CHICHESTER, WEST SUSSEX
Copyright © 1989 Columbia University Press
All rights reserved

LIBRARY OF CONGRESS
CATALOGING-IN-PUBLICATION DATA
Schlesinger, James R.
America at century's end / James Schlesinger.
p. cm.
"Radner lectures"—P. v.
Includes index.
ISBN 0-231-06922-7
1. United States—Politics and government—1981–1989.
2. United States—Politics and government—1989–
3. United States—Foreign relations—1981–1989.
4. United States—Foreign relations—1989–
I. Title. II. Title: Radner lectures.
E876.S35 1989
320.973—dc19   89-30700
CIP

Printed in the United States of America

Casebound editions of Columbia University Press books
are printed on permanent and
durable acid-free paper
c 10 9 8 7 6 5 4 3 2

THE RADNER LECTURES

★

IN 1956 the Radner Family Foundation established a
lectureship at Columbia University in memory of William Radner, a graduate of Columbia College and the
Columbia Law School. Since his career in the public
service had been terminated by his untimely death, the
gift appropriately stipulated that these lectures were to
deal with subjects in the field of public law and government. Previous Radner Lectures were:

1959   Harry S. Truman, former President of the United
       States
       The Presidency
1960   Lord Boothby, Rector of the University of St.
       Andrew's
       *Parliament and the Profession of Politics in Brit-
       ain*

1963   Robert R. Bowie, Director of the Center for International Affairs, and Dillon Professor of International Relations, Harvard University
Present and Future in Foreign Policy

1965   Lord Harlech, Former British Ambassador to the United States
Must the West Decline?

1966   Richard E. Neustadt, Professor of Government and Associate Dean in the John F. Kennedy School of Government, Harvard University
Alliance Politics

1972   Robert C. Wood, former President of the University of Massachusetts
The Necessary Majority: Middle America and the Urban Crisis

CONTENTS

★

(vii)

PREFACE

★

IT SHOULD be self-evident, but it also should be une-
quivocally stated at the outset, how honored and grate-
ful I am that the president and trustees of Columbia
University chose me to be the William Radner lecturer
for 1988. This illustrious institution traces its history to
well before the inception of our Republic. Its contributions to American scholarship are well known. So I am
delighted—if only for a fleeting moment—to join in its
academic procession.

AMERICA AT CENTURY'S END

I

★

The Setting:
What America
is Like

HE RADNER Lectures were established in 1956. Their intent was "to advance understanding of government, broadly conceived." The date is noteworthy— for it helps to explain the intent. It was a period marked by American preeminence, and a dawning consciousness in this society of that preeminence. Until that time there had, perhaps, been insufficient recognition of the permanence of America's international role and, therefore, the permanence of *government* responsibility.

The expansion of the government during the 1930s might be viewed as temporary, reflecting the need to respond to the depression and the widespread unemployment. The further expansion of government during World War II might also be viewed as temporary, reflecting the obvious requirement to defeat powerful foes at the opposite sides of the Atlantic and Pacific oceans. Many, however, regarded that expansion as both abnormal and transitory. Surely when the war ended, we could go home. Indeed, we tried to. We brought the boys home, and largely disbanded the armed forces. You here at Columbia made America's war hero, Dwight Eisenhower, into *your* president—and transformed him into a civilian. (By making him your president you both anticipated and led the country by just a few years.) Without the simplicity, not to say ignorance, that marked President Harding, we too sought, at least in thought, a return to "normalcy."

The year 1956 was a year of revelation—of the deeper structural changes that had occurred in the world. It was the year of the Anglo-French-Israeli invasion of Egypt in the attempt to seize or, if you will, reclaim the Suez Canal. Simultaneously it represented an attempt by the European states to reassert some of their prewar power. After all, Britain had been one of the wartime Big Three and France was at least a nominal victor. But with the intervention of the Soviet Union and the United States, the true shift in world power stood starkly revealed. When Mr. Khrushchev, in his characteristically boisterous manner, threatened to "rain missiles down on London and Paris," it was the United States that had to move in to protect its friends and allies—these former great powers. It was the United States that had to order Mr. Khruschev to get back into his box—and to content himself with his spoils in Hungary. For better or worse, it was also American policy that ordained the Anglo-French failure to Suez. The French were angry and resentful; being French they nursed their distrust of the United States, which tells us much about the subsequent attitudes of Gaullist France. The British were angry and distressed; being British they were also resigned, drawing their own conclusion about the shift of power. Harold MacMillan, leader of the same Britain that had been the leading world power for almost two centuries, succinctly stated (or understated) the implications for Europe. "Over to you," was his comment to the Americans as the full shift of power became visible.

It is perhaps symbolic of the underlying motivations that led to the establishment of the Radner Lectures that the first lecturer was none other than former President Harry S. Truman. While in office, Mr. Truman had been a notable transition figure. He had presided over a vast international watershed, a period of distinctive and deep-seated change—without fully grasping how fundamental those changes had been. In many ways Mr. Truman had been a political figure who carried forward the visceral impulses of the prewar period. He recognized neither the immense weight that the United States had acquired, nor the inability to shuck off many of the burdens thus acquired. He was inclined to believe that, while avoiding some of the mistakes of the post-World War I isolationism of the 1920s, nevertheless the United States could to a large extent disengage. After all, it was

Mr. Truman who demobilized the armed forces. It was Mr. Truman who, within a few days of the end of the war, terminated Lend-Lease. Only after the passage of several years (and under the guidance of figures like George Marshall and Dean Acheson) did Mr. Truman accomplish the great deeds for which he is renown— the Marshall Plan, the Berlin Airlift, the NATO Alliance, and the like. In brief, that first William Radner lecturer thus represented both that slowly unfolding awareness of the dramatically new international role for the United States and that need for extended and *permanent* government involvement which had motivated the establishment of the Radner Lectures.

It is my intention to fulfill the purposes of the founders "to advance the understanding of government" by drawing on my own quarter-century observations of an intimate involvement in government. There is considerable insight in Yogi Berra's unintended aphorism: "one can observe a lot, by just watching."

I hope to deal with some fundamental aspects of governance in the American society and to do so at an academically respectable level of generalization. I shall avoid the grubby details—the now-it-can-be-tolds and who-struck-Johns—which, not infrequently, is the source of considerable interest, not to say titillation. In short, I shall not provide the spicy details that excite a prurient interest, and I trust that there are only a few journalists among you who will be disappointed.

I shall begin with my observation of the special nature

of the American society. With all the talk of American "exceptionalism," it remains quite clear that the nature of that exceptionalism is not widely understood. America is not as exceptional, as all too many believe, in somehow being exempt from the economic, political, and military constraints that ultimately must limit the freedom of action of any society. (Indeed one of the elements of American exceptionalism may be the belief —or the hope—that through the Grace of God this country is so exempt.)

Yet America is exceptional—in the sense that its history, its assumptions, and its attitudes are quite different from those European societies that gave it birth. Those attitudes both reflect and contribute to the greater freedom of action that the United States has enjoyed, most notably in foreign policy. And those differences make it difficult for our allies and our opponents to understand us, for they too are inclined to judge us in accordance with their own presuppositions.

I shall next develop how these special characteristics of the American society affect in turn foreign policy and domestic policy.

For now, however, let me deal with the special characteristics of this country: WHAT AMERICA IS LIKE. It is crucial, as a first priority, to examine this question. It underlies that special American style in foreign policy, so confusing to friend and foe, that is certainly unique among those nations that have become great or dominant powers. Foreign policy in the American society is not and cannot be some abstract embodiment of the national interest. Generations of scholars and, for sure, most foreign observers have either erred in this quest or, at best, pursued an ideal that is irrelevant. A sharp and lasting definition of the national interest depends upon authority, which in turn depends upon hierarchy —two ingredients that have marked most societies in history, of which America is preciously short.

Among the relevant set of societies, America is unique in that is has virtually no feudal past. The relations among free individuals are based on volunteerism and not upon reciprocal obligation. What little social structure or hierarchy this country inherited, primarily in the Eastern states, was notably diluted in the nineteenth century, particularly after the Civil War, under the impact of new wealth—and then substantially disappeared after World War II, reflecting both the greater social freedom and the reduced power of the East coast.

One result is a very modest respect for authority. First visitors to the United States are regularly amazed at the disregard, if not disrespect, in which American citizens hold authority. Even our Canadian neighbors, in a society so much more placid, are perplexed. It should not be forgotten that the American nation was born in the rejection of authority—the authority of the British crown. The United States is not a nation in the European sense of the term. Its people are not bound together by (largely) common ethnic background and historic experience, almost immemorial. Instead, as

Samuel Huntington has observed, it is a nation "defined in terms of documents," the Declaration of Independence and the Constitution. Its sense of community is therefore not, as elsewhere, simply an inheritance, but is based upon the central force of adherence to the American creed.

Rejection of authority makes the American rather feisty. I recall a memoir in *The New Yorker* that illustrates the point. It was by an American, who had spent the wartime period in England, and was finally returning home. His words, if I can recall them, were roughly as follows: "when I first boarded the SS *America* at Southampton, I knew that I was once again in the Land of the Free. I asked a steward the way to my cabin. He jerked his thumb over his shoulder at a sign, with numbers, on the wall, and said, 'Whatsamatter, Bub, can't you read?'" The American's instinctive response to a demand for deference to authority: "in a pig's eye."

In this most truly democratic of democratic societies, public opinion rules. Without the continuing support of public opinion, there can be no stability in policy. I have just mentioned that, contrary to the expectations of many scholars and statesman, foreign policy does not rest upon some abstract definition of the national interest. It rests on public opinion. Similarly, *and contrary to what their supporters may suggest,* even popular presidents—presidents elected in landslides—are not free to determine foreign policy. Presidents, who disregard public opinion, do so at their own peril.

Not only can public opinion be quite volatile, but Americans are rather changeable, some might say excitable. In the United States the Tides of Fashion can alter with astonishing suddenness. It was George Santayana who so well delineated this country. "America," he said, "is a vast prairie swept by one universal bonfire." Of you who have reflected the recent rise and fall of Ollie-mania will recognize the speed with which enthusiasm can wax and wane. Such vicissitudes of public opinion in the United States may make it difficult to achieve a firm base for policy.

Changing fashions and an unwillingness to defer to authority mean that the United States is not very good at learning from experience. Actions, learned in the past to be in error, are likely to be repeated. The wag who observed, "the only thing that we learn from history is that we learn nothing from history" is likely to have had this country in mind.

The ultimate purpose of this society is to preserve the people's freedom. That freedom will not be inhibited, save by constitutional constraints. Yet the preservation of freedom, including the freedom to change, is scarcely the ideal basis of *stable* policy. While this may be quite acceptable, even desirable in domestic policy, by contrast, in foreign policy, in which continuity is so important an element, especially for the leading world power, the predilection for freedom of action over stability of policy can cause serious problems.

The Constitution represents, of course, an element of

stability. But the Constitution also preserves within itself the potential for instabilities. It is an eighteenth-century constitution, based upon an older English model that in the mother country has gradually been superseded. It is based upon the separation of powers. (Indeed the authors of the Constitution had anticipated, or feared, that the legislative branch would be the dominant one.) Moreover, the separation of powers rests upon the presupposition that, unless agreement can be forged between the two branches, it is preferable not to move toward new policies. Such a belief may have been appropriate for an America which was largely detached from international involvement and which sought a government of limited powers. For reasons that are obvious it is the source of continuing, indeed increasing, uneasiness in the latter part of the twentieth century.

The only way in which the American system can effectively perform is when policy is based upon *consensus*. In the absence of consensus, the system can perform quite poorly. Thus, the highest art for the statesman in the American system of government is the forging of consensus. The demanding requirement for creating consensus is inherent in the American system of governance. Nonetheless in recent years we have had difficulty in understanding this elementary point. Why is that? Older Americans, those whose expectations were shaped in the period of World War II and the subsequent cold war, came of age in a period that was novel and almost unique in American history. In the 1930s, as was true of much of our history, there were deep divisions over American policy. It was Pearl Harbor that swept away those divisions and created an instant national consensus. In World War II the American society was fully united in the quest to defeat those universally regarded as evil foes. Contrast that view with those in the Vietnam War, the Mexican War, the Spanish-American War, and (in the North) even the Civil War. Total national unity is the exceptional experience in this country, yet such unity became the expectation for a generation of Americans. Save for a small minority the consensus continued through much of the cold war.

What was equally important, though in a sense a corollary, was the long persisting willingness of the U.S. Congress to defer to the president on foreign policy matters. For more that twenty-five years, from Pearl Harbor roughly to the time of the Tet offensive in Vietnam, a president could rely upon the Congress, despite grumbling, to follow his lead.

Since the late 1960s, that has all changed. We have returned to a more normal condition of the American Democracy—in which national unity on foreign policy matters cannot be assumed. Automatic deference by the Congress to the executive is gone. Indeed, during the difficult years of the 1970s, the Congress seemed to enjoy asserting its independence by defying and thwarting various presidents. Yet, while the hostility of the seventies may have diminished, the deference of the fifties clearly has not returned.

For many, including myself, who have served in the executive branch, the relationships in those good old days were right and fitting—the natural order of things. I sympathize with that view, but it is irrelevant. The congressional deference to the executive that marked that era has disappeared—along with the national consensus that existed in that era. Short of a clear and unequivocal national emergency, like Pearl Harbor itself, such deference by the Congress to the executive is unlikely to return. Frustrating as it might be to many who serve in government, grappling with national divisions over policy may be our normal lot. The executive can lead only through persuasion. That is never an easy task. It should not expect deference, even though such a relationship is understandably more comfortable.

Like it or not, the foreign policy agencies of the executive branch must accept that they now operate in a new context in dealing with the Congress. Many of those who serve in them—probably a majority—do not like it. Some—happily a minority—resist accepting these altered conditions. Either in the long run or in the short, a failure to accept those changes will limit their agency's ability to do its job. No agency can forgo congressional support. The widespread nostalgia within the executive branch for an idealized world that is now past, indeed a world that never was, is not only irrelevant, it is both counterproductive and false.

There is a graffitto that is germane: "even nostalgia ain't what it used to be." That idealized world never existed even in the halcyon days of apparently total congressional branch deference. Even in the good old days, congressional approval was required—and need not be forthcoming. Methods of consultation might be limited to a very few leaders and might be far more private. But it is purely false nostalgia to believe that Congress, in some sense, was a pushover. In those days, if Richard Russell or Sam Rayburn (two illustrious examples) said no, *it was no*.

Obtaining congressional acquiescence has always been and continues to be, indispensable. On larger policy matters it is obligatory to forge consensus. While the task may have become harder and involve many more people than it did in postwar period, the task itself is not a novelty. It is not only an error, but an error incorporating a large degree of naivete, to believe that one can run roughshod over the Congress. I can well recall the admonitions of Bryce Harlow, that gifted and perceptive executive branch giant of small stature. Bryce, who stood about five-foot-four in his stockinged feet, used to insist that when he first came to Washington he had stood six-foot-five inches, but then had been gradually worn down. Before serving in the White House for several presidents, Harlow had served on Capitol Hill. He was one of the keenest observers and wittiest expositors of the realities of the American government and the ways of Washington life.

Early in the Nixon years, after listening for a period to newcomers to Washington, most prominently from southern California, speak contemptuously about the Congress, Harlow warned them, more or less in the following words. "All right, I understand that the Congress is disorganized and frequently inconsistent. I also understand that many members of the Congress are not especially endowed with brains. But do not make the mistake of complacently calling the Congress stupid and believing that you can ignore it. Just remember this: whatever you may think of the intelligence of those in the Congress, the Congress has immense power. If you provoke it sufficently, it can rear back and strike you. It can destroy an administration. Never underestimate the Congress." In retrospect, I regard Harlow's words as one of history's great, if understated, prophetic comments.

It is no secret that intelligence operations are inherently a matter of special sensitivity. It is no secret that some in the intelligence community, including a recent Director of Central Intelligence, have found the new oversight procedures, established by the Congress in the late 1970s, to be burdensome and highly unwelcome. It is also no secret, that there have been attempts to evade those oversight procedures and, if necessary, deceive the Oversight Committees in the process. From time to time there has been support for such attitudes within the White House Staff. Within the last eighteen months, these tendencies have come to a head in the so-called Iran Contra affair. That affair has shed additional light on the dangers for the executive branch in attempting to run roughshod over the Congress. After listening to the highly revealing disquisitions on constitutional government by both Colonel North and Admiral Poindexter, I did come to one firm conclusion: we need to do a better job teaching the Constitution at Annapolis— that very Constitution that professional military officers must take an oath to support and defend.

Whenever an administration experiences a serious setback, there will be a spreading demand for new procedures to prevent a recurrence. The word serious, in this context refers to political salience, stretching all the way from substantively weighty matters such as arms for the Ayatollah Khomeini to substantively insignificant, though politically visible, issues like high-priced monkey wrenches and toilet seats. For the most part, the quest for new procedures reflects a touching American belief that more oversight, more consultation, more people in the loop, more layers of appeal, will more or less miraculously preclude error or skulduggery. But miracle-working is not part of the bureaucratic routine. There remains a profound, if disquieting, truth: in government there is no substitute for sensible men with an understanding for sensible policies.

Contrary to a deeply held American conviction, wider discussion does not mean better discussion. Procedures provide no substitute for substance. While procedures may somewhat alleviate the risk of doing something wrong, procedures may well create other problems. Procedures are likely to cause delays, either natural or deliberate. Such procedures provide an invaluable instrument for those in the system who wish to undermine either a policy or the process by which it is arrived at. In short, procedures may reduce the risk of errors of commission—but only at the price of increasing the risk of errors of omission. Elsewhere in the world there is less confidence that procedures by themselves can substitute for substance. It is a rather special American conviction, reflecting no doubt a disregard for knowledge and for authority, that there is always some kind of management trick that will solve our problems.

The fundamental point—one impossible to evade—is that government requires talent. This would seem to be elementary. But in a society that from time to time professes to despise government what is elementary may be forgotten. If government is treated as useless or worse, if civil servants are neglected or abused, the ultimate impact on policy making is foreordained. If it is widely believed that "government is not the solution; government is the problem," then inevitably government will become the problem. It is a self-fulfilling prophecy. Whether it be an appropriate form of poetic justice or a tragedy: in a democracy, the public gets the kind of government it deserves.

As one examines the American system, relations between the executive and Congress, and performance in the executive branch, one must inevitably come to the president. Since we have just completed the Bicentennial celebration, we should bear in mind that the makers of the Constitution, meeting in Philadelphia two hundred years ago, were not simply designing an office based on general principles of political theory. The office of president was specifically designed with George Washington in mind. Washington not only enjoyed towering prestige, he was without question the most experienced leader in the land. Few of Washington's successors can be said to be first in war and first in peace; more may be said to be first in the hearts of their countrymen.

In my judgment there is no substitute for experience in a president. But it is rare to get an Eisenhower or a Nixon with broad experience in foreign policy. More frequently, one gets a Johnson or a Ford, legislators whose primary experience is in domestic affairs; and recently, we have had outsiders, governors like Carter or Reagan, who come to the office as total novices in the operation of the federal government. Indeed, as head of government the office is unique in the free world. No apprenticeship is required—odd as that may seem. As a result the office is regularly filled with legislative men, academic men, and what may be called natural men, those who follow their own impulses. Once again, this is not wholly reassuring regarding the kind of judgment and experience required in foreign policy.

Within an administration one will encounter what is either a habit of mind or a battle cry: all power resides in the president. That tends to be the refrain of the White House staff, the executive office, and even the executive branch at large. Members of executive departments and agencies will walk up the prerogatives of the president in dealing with outsiders, notably the Hill. However they will be notably less inclined to do so in talking to the White House staff or the agencies within the executive office. As one might infer, this theme that all power resides in the president is employed as a weapon, with the intent to convey implication that *I* am closer to the president than *thou*. Within the White House staff, it is played with considerable fervor and sometimes with remarkable skill. But that theme is not only a weapon, it also represents a seductive trap for those who employ it.

Reality is rather different from the refrain. In reality the Office of the President inherently (i.e., constitutionally) a rather weak one. It embodies far less power than the public believes. It does provide a "bully pulpit," but only for those who can use it. Fundamentally the power of the office lies less in its Constitutional prerogatives than in the ability to persuade. That is no small power, however, in a society in which public opinion rules— and in which the president can dominate communications and the media. Nonetheless, the reality is that a president requires support and cooperation. President Nixon used to enjoin his subordinates in government, "you've got to bring your people along." Those that "must be brought along" number in the many hundreds —members of Congress, and key officials, and beyond them opinion-makers and the media.

In my judgment there is a principal, if rather unpleasant, responsibility to remind a president of the limitations of this power. The president's aides must help him correctly to channel his energies. The White House staff must, in a sense, hem him in; it must "force" him to listen to advice. And that is likely to go against the grain of the legislative or academic or natural man, who has brought his distinct, if not always relevant, views to the office.

If the White House staff is performing a service for the president it will focus on what is do-able. It will not focus on what is merely flattering; that is, what may *theoretically* lie within the president's constitutional powers. If the White House staff is rendering proper service, it will, above all, provide frank talk and engender restraint. It will not simply do what the president thinks he wants, because the staff believes that he wants it. Thus, the staffs' duty is to remind the president of his limitations.

For this purpose quite regularly, the White House staff is anything but an asset. One danger is that the staff will simply flatter the president regarding his influence and his power. A more insidious danger is that the White House staff will itself come to believe the message it conveys. The staff will then reassure the president that all his problems are external. The president will be encouraged to believe that the real problems lie, not with his goals or with his strategy and tactics, but rather out there—in the departments and agencies, in the Congress, or in the press. If the White House staff encourages such illusions, it clearly is not an asset.

The White House as an institution, is peculiarly susceptible to various forms of psychological disorders. When things are going well for the president and the administration, the White House becomes vulnerable to hubris, the belief that the president cannot fail and can do no wrong. In that psychological state a president will be induced to overreach. Any list of successes, but, most notably, landslide elections, as in 1964, 1972, and 1984, will feed White House hubris—with potentially baleful effects for the president's standing.

By contrast, when things are going badly, the institution will likely succumb to a greater or lesser degree to paranoia. Invariably the paranoia will focus on the press, though the Congress is always a good competitor. While the level of psychological distress within the White House will vary over time and in accordance with a president's disposition and style, the institution always is subject to one of these two disorders—and will tend to oscillate between them.

George Reedy, in his forceful and insightful book somewhat misleadingly entitled *The Twilight of the Presidency*, dissected some of these problems with the presidency as an institution. His book demands careful study by all those concerned with governance in America. As might be expected, some of his observations reflect the special characteristics of the Johnson White

House, but many of the problems he pointed out are far more general. The isolation of the president, the co-coon-like protection that may preclude his coming in contact with reality appear to be increasing problems. The president is increasingly surrounded by his own "creatures and creations"—and has reduced contact with those who might speak more objectively to him. Flattery is omnipresent, not only explicit flattery but, the implicit flattery that pervades the atmosphere of the White House and its various entourages.

In this light I can do no better than to quote these observations by Reedy: "The most important, and least examined problem of the presidency is that of maintaining contact with reality. . . . A president's most persistent problem in staying in touch with reality lies in his staff. . . . it is the creature of the president, a group of men who have one purpose in life and one purpose only —to perform personal services for the man in charge."

Even a century ago, in a day of lesser attentiveness and fewer creature comforts, Lord Bryce pointed out in his *American Commonwealth* that the White House was simply a court. Sheer sycophancy is no more unknown in the White House than it is in any other court. Readers of St. Simon's reminiscences about the Court of Louis XIV would not find behavior in the White House entirely unfamiliar. There is no ultimate cure for the problem. There are only palliatives. The strongest antidote—probably the only antidote—is the self-restraint and modesty that the president himself may bring to the White House. If he lacks a sense of self-restraint when he comes to the White House, there is nothing in the environment that will provide it for him.

I myself have spent a little time in the White House, more in the executive office, but most of my time has been spent in the departments and agencies of the executive branch. My view, not wholly neutral, reflects that experience. As, no doubt, can be seen, I am not, in general, a fan of the White House staff. I am particularly suspicious of an "overbloated" White House staff. I fully recognize that a president must have his own trusted aides, with no bureaucratic loyalties other than to him, with whom he can immediately communicate. A small high-quality staff is indispensable for coordinating the government.

My problem grows as the White House staff expands. With that expansion comes competition with respect to areas of responsibility and competition for the attention of the president. As numbers and rivalry increase, White House aides begin to generate their own business, bringing into the White House problems which, from the president's standpoint, would better be left to the departments and agencies and not become his responsibility. White House aides begin to develop and then expand their own agendas. The inevitable result is to set White House staff in rivalry with the departments and agencies. Almost invariably the president will be obliged to devote steadily more time to his own staff and correspondingly less time to the problems out there in the executive branch.

General Brent Scowcroft, who has served effectively several presidents in the White House, has stressed the need for the White House staff to provide a "presidential" perspective on those problems that are "presidential." What General Scowcroft states is certainly correct. But it is equally true that the staff needs to refrain from imposing a presidential perspective on those problems that are not presidental. For the White House staff to be useful to the president, it must be part of the solution rather than part of the problem.

In my view it is important that the White House staff not be permitted to substitute for the departments and agencies. The departments and agencies should be allowed to perform their own functions. They are out there, where as the saying goes, the rubber meets the road. They know better what the substantive problems are than does the White House staff. They understand the reactions of the public and of the relevant constituencies, and they have a better feel for the congressional mood. Moreover, the departments and agencies have, not only the resources, but the understanding to operate in those areas of responsibility with which they are charged. More frequently than not, attempts by the White House staff to preempt problems, and to "take charge" will occur without either sufficient knowledge or sufficient resources—and with results that may be comic or unfortunate, if not disastrous. Aggrandizement by elements of the White House staff remain a potential menace to the president. While a few spectacular successes may be achieved (and inevitably become part of the White House folklore), over the long run the costs invariably are too high.

To place such continuing weight on the cabinet departments has implications for the cabinet officers and their selection. It should not be necessary to state, but regrettably it is, that the cabinet officers should be chosen for their competency and talent—and not for old connections, campaign contributions, cronyism, or locker-room good fellowship. But it is also essential that the president has reasonably good rapport with cabinet members. He should be prepared to deal with them face-to-face on important issues. The relationship should be straightforward. Both he and they should be able to lay their cards on the table. The benefits of such a relationship are clear. There will be less suspicion both of and on the part of cabinet officers. Consequently there will be much less opportunity for middle-man dealing. No system can work effectively if there are behind-the-scenes Svengalis intruding into areas that are not their responsibility.

It is now time to draw some conclusion and better to relate how government operates to what America is like. Therefore let me close with two trends of recent years that, by altering the American society, have affected the performance of government. I refer to two recent devel-

opments. First is the change in society's behavior induced by the powerful medium of television. Second is
the increasing precedence that electoral politics take
over the functions of government. Needless to say, these
changes, are interrelated. And both simultaneouly reflect and contribute to the loss of consensus on substantive issues and the continuity of government policy.

Let me start with television, the medium that has
reshaped the nation's social and political landscape. That
TV would be a major force was, and was recognized to
be inevitable. But only a few, such as Marshall
McLuhan, foresaw how dramatic and qualitatively different would be the impact of the new medium. Television has superseded to a significant extent other forces
in shaping *the public mind*. To be sure, its *direct* impact
on leadership groups (a.k.a. "elites") is substantially less.
The elites go on talking about television's shallowness
and distortions, and may go on bristling about "the vast
wasteland," as former FCC Chairman Newton Minow
called it. Some make a fettish of refusing to watch it at
all—"a waste of time."

The point is that the general public simply does not
care about such reservations. The public finds television
to be a perfectly satisfactory form of entertainment and
a provider of information adequate to its needs. (Those
are not entirely separate phenomena.) The public forms
its impressions of individual politicians through the medium. TV has to a large extent superseded family, political party, church, and even to some extent social group-

ings as a way of shaping the voters' attitudes toward political figures and political issues.

I have said earlier that in the American democracy public opinion determines policy. In the past the voters were somewhat more timid in individually reaching judgments about, say, the specifics of foreign policy. They would rely more on outside sources of authority— political party, union, church, a favorite newspaper. No longer.

Television makes it easy for the voter directly to form an impression or a final judgment. Much of the public has limited ability and even less confidence in verbalization. There is no great desire to sift through mere words, particularly the written word. Under these conditions it is no surprise that, in electoral impact, TV comes like rain to a parched desert. The voter can form his own impression directly. He can substitute for or supplement mere words with a visual impression. To whatever extent he wishes, he can "eyeball" the candidates. He can watch their body language, he can form an impression—accurate, or inaccurate, but satisfactory to him—of the candidates he is asked to vote for.

At the time of the Cuban Missile crisis, when U-2 aircraft first brought back aerial photographs of Soviet construction activity, it was stated simply but eloquently: "A picture is worth a thousand words." That is certainly true in intelligence matters. But it is also true in political matters generally. The sight of Alexander Haig in a moment of national distress stating "I'm in charge here" makes a more indelible impact than all the services and words of the general. The *sight* of Robert Dole in a delicate moment after the New Hampshire primary stating about George Bush: "tell him to stop lying about my record" similarly makes an indelible impression. For better or for worse, the public's impression of men's characters are formed by such brief episodes—if on camera. One wonders whether, if Jimmy Carter had confessed that he "lusted after women in his heart" *on tape* rather than in the pages of a magazine, he would have been elected president in the first place.

Public opinion determines policy, and with TV the public has found an instrument with which in can form *on its own* judgments in which it can have confidence. Television shapes the public's judgments on issues as well as men. Pictures on TV did more to form the public's judgment on the Vietnam War than half a billion words in the Congress. The public mind is to an extraordinary degree shaped by TV. To change a public impression etched by TV is probably no easier than to alter the tides.

The rise of television has buttressed the traditional skepticism of freeborn American citizens regarding "authority." If one can form one's own opinion directly, one has even less need for the knowledge or the views of experts. That has contributed to the reduced status within the American society of universities, whose standing with the public reached a peak during the late '50s and early '60s. Since the diminished stature may be a somewhat delicate subject with this audience, let me cite the words of one who may be judged more sympathetic, and perhaps more authoritative, Steven Muller, the president of Johns Hopkins University.

> If greatness is equated with national stature, then part of the problem with today's university presidents may be that we are not media personalities. In a society whose attention span has shrunk from earlier times and that reads less and less, national recognition derives primarily from national television. On the one hand, the thoughtful address, the detailed exposition of the complicated have been largely replaced by one-liners and headlines. On the other hand, prolonged and repeated national television exposure has elevated to national stature (greatness?) not only politicians but also television commentators, articulate athletes, and other entertainers. University presidents are not —most of us—show biz.

But what is true of university presidents tends also to be true of other skilled and trained professionals. That, definitely, includes those who serve the government, whether they be foreign service officers, budget experts, military officers, or intelligence experts. And those who are put in charge of them are deemed to have less need of knowledge and expertise than was true some decades ago or, let us say, at the time that the Radner Lectures were established.

This brings me to my second and final point, which can be stated simply. I refer to the rise of electoral politics and its tendency to overshadow governance. Electoral politics is fun. Government is hard and unremitting work. In a sense that has always been true. However in the last three elections the focus has been on the zest of campaigning itself rather than what will be done when one has taken power. Campaigns grow longer and longer, and those not especially drawn to the joys of campaigning (or, more precisely, those who cannot easily endure the agonies of campaigning) become less likely to reach high office.

The effect of the increasing tendency of electoral politics to subordinate actual government is to lessen respect for government itself. This has been reinforced since the Watergate episode by outsiders running for president against either Washington or government or both. Such campaigns can hardly engender a high respect for government. Nor, may I add, will they engender high respect for those who serve in government or for the talents that they may possess or require.

I have referred earlier to the erosion of the political consensus that dominated foreign policy from Pearl Harbor to Tet. Thus, from a unique period in American history of consensus we have returned to our normal political divisions. Needless to say, that evolution has increased political needs relative to professional needs.

That has also been reinforced by the volatility of American politics, the rise of TV, and a public opinion, not only *inherently* dominant, but more assertive on the details of policy. All this has reduced the appreciation for and the role of trained professionals in serving the government. That tendency in turn has been reinforced by a rise in ideological fervor, which directly suggests that the convictions of a true believer represents are a higher qualification for office than professional knowledge, experience, or mere competency.

I trust that it is not superfluous for me to add that I regard such a trend as unfortunate.

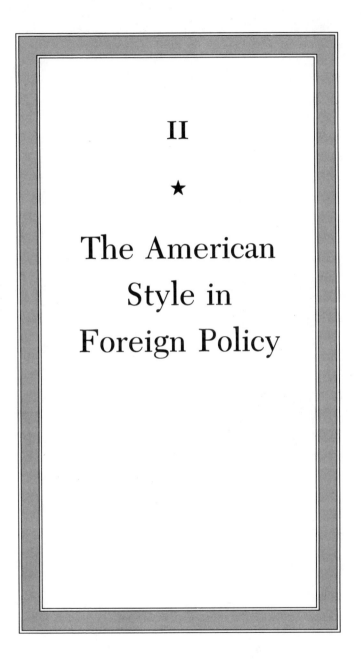

II

★

The American
Style in
Foreign Policy

S PART of our examination of American government and society, I want to explore the special American style in foreign policy. I shall do so first by picking up again certain themes on What America Is Like, and then by developing those themes later.

It was axiomatic that one could not examine this nation's foreign policy until one better understood what this country was like. There have been many, scholars and European observers for the most part, who have implicitly assumed that a nation's foreign policy can be designed more or less in abstraction from the *social* context. They have provided precepts drawn from European experience, though not explicitly acknowledged to be so. They have dealt with something called the national interest, as if that national interest were self evident. From time to time American leaders have been drawn into such abstractions, not infrequently to their own ultimate distress.

To be sure, the national interest is a relevant concept, but it is not a sure guide to policy formation. To be sure, European experience is relevant. But precepts drawn from European experience cannot be transferred directly to the United States. Those who attempt to do so will misunderstand both the foundations of and the motivating forces behind American foreign policy.

In describing this Republic, I touched on four points particularly relevant to American foreign policy, which I wish to review. First, American history is special. It is quite different from the history of other great powers. Unlike the European states it does not have a feudal past, gradually giving way to nationalism—a process well underway by the sixteenth century. Indeed this country was settled for the most part by those who chose to leave European shores. The nation was born in rebellion against European authority—the authority of the British crown.

Perhaps the most influential of these groups of settlers were the Puritans. Their attitudes were particularly influential in shaping the national psyche and the subsequent development of the nation. In part, this reflected the willingness of New Englanders to work hard at indoctrination. In part, it reflected the historic constraints on the South, that other and initially stronger source of leadership. Those constraints reflecting the "peculiar institution," slavery, the Civil War, military subjugation, and a lengthy period of subordination, most markedly in the period of Republican dominance after the Civil War. The South was so eager simply to be left alone that it did not seek, for a lengthy period, to shape the nation's psyche.

What the Puritans bequeathed to this country was a sense of mission. It was the Puritans who believed, indeed, felt to the very core of their beings, that America was destined to be a "beacon unto the nations." Clearly that belief in its original Calvinist manifestation faded away, but almost as clearly it has continued to influence generations of Americans with a deep conviction that, in its international role, America has a mission.

Even for those whom we now call isolationists, there was a deep-seated belief, perhaps most eloquently expressed by the elder LaFollette, that through perfection in isolation of its own society America would better serve other nations by providing a model and guide. This was a later and secularized version of Governor John Winthrop's "the City Shining on the Hill"—a vision mixing poetry and mysticism that President Reagan would revive with intent more narrowly patriotic. And, quite clearly, during the more recent periods of American international engagement, that belief in America's mission has been more forceful and forthright. Victory in two world wars, and particularly the second World War, gave America the opportunity to attempt to reshape the world in its own image. While this has not been a total success (inevitably other nations could not fully enter into the American enthusiasm that they become more like us), nonetheless, both the fervent belief and the quest were there.

Indeed, that conviction was there even in rather more ambiguous circumstances. According to his memoirs, William McKinley spent a sleepless night prayerfully considering whether despite Spain's willingness to negotiate all areas of difference, the United States should declare war on Spain. He determined to do so on the basis that it was America's historic duty "to christianize the natives" of the Philippines, oblivious of the somewhat inconvenient fact that they had been substantially Catholic for two centuries.

America's geographic isolation has been critical in determining American attitudes—both the long term, if oscillating, isolationist impulse and the vision of America as the role model for the world. Since the War of 1812, the simple fact is that America, until the advent of Soviet nuclear capabilities, has had no serious external threat. The Germans in World War I might engage in unrestricted submarine warfare. The Japanese in World War II may have lobbed a few shells onto American soil, seized Attu, and even threatened the Hawaiian islands. In that war once again German submarines, operating close to our coasts, may have threatened the tanker movement of oil. Nonetheless, since the Battle of New Orleans, there has not been a serious threat to the continental United States. The few foes that we faced on North American soil, starting with the Indians, could be dealt with summarily—if somewhat harshly.

All this gave rise to a sense of invulnerability, probably unique among modern states. Perhaps the Japanese before 1945 had a vaguely similar sense of invulnerability. Perhaps the Tibetans for rather different reasons may have felt the same thing. But certainly not the European states, all of which had periodically been overrun by their neighbors. Even the Russians, with a deep-seated conviction that Russia could ultimately survive invasion, had no sense of invulnerability. Certainly neither the Canadians or the Mexicans could have such a sense. The United States stands alone in the way that its history and geography have shaped a belief in the natural, if not God-given, invulnerabilty of the United States. It is a belief buried deep in the American psyche that this is the natural order of things. As we shall see later this continues to have consequences.

The second point was that in the United States, this democracy of democracies, public opinion constrains and determines foreign policy. Of course in other states public opinion can be disregarded only at risk to the regime. No public ultimately will fail to repudiate failure. No great power can for long be effective unless it has the support, even if it be weak and tacit, of the populace.

A Richelieu or a Bismarck really needed only the support of his monarch. Such men could make decisions, running against the grain of instinctive public desires, so long as his policies were crowned with a modicum of success. He could look to the longer run— indeed, the longer term national interest. Public opinion imposed far less constraint on his choices. He was not obliged to worry about sustaining short-term public support. In brief, unlike the United States, public opinion did not dominate.

By contrast, in the United States, policy in a sense wells up from below. Unless a policy has public support it will ultimately fail. Indeed, policy may well up from below in a more direct sense. An administration can, against its own wishes, be overwhelmed by public opinion—as in the dissolution of our efforts in Southeast Asia or in the imposition of sanctions in South Africa. Such formation-from-below of foreign policy may not be the normal order of things. But, if they are to prosper, all American leaders must understand one thing: a prerequisite for any serious American policy is that the American people be engaged.

American leaders who attempt to construct foreign policies that lack the support of the public are doomed to frustration. This ultimately proved to be true for both President Johnson and President Nixon in Vietnam. But the public can be as hostile to noble visions as to war, for it was equally true after World War I for President Wilson, when he unsuccessfully sought to engage the American society in the League of Nations. The most effective leaders—a Roosevelt or an Eisenhower—understand the need to remain constantly in touch with the public mood. President Reagan came to understand that he had little public support in Lebanon and, realistically though I believe reluctantly, withdrew American forces. President Carter failed to understand the disinclination of his countrymen to turn the other cheek regarding Ayatollah Khomeini's Iran—and paid dearly for it. Unless a foreign policy enjoys public support, it is, to borrow a Marxist expression, "adventurist." While public support does not ensure foreign policy success (in the absense of which such public support will fade), the lack of public support for a major adventure ensures failure.

A third point to recall: foreign policymaking has become *increasingly* subject to mass opinion; it is *increasingly* democratic. This may be attributed to a variety of interlocking influences. Vastly improved communications, including both television and polling, has meant that the public receives information (or misinformation) and forms and conveys its views far more rapidly than hitherto. Elected officials, notably members of Congress, are more susceptible to such changes in public opinion. Deviations in their votes from strong preferences among their constituents will be reported more quickly and viewed more searchingly. The weakening of party structures and of regular party voting among constituents reduce protection from the pressures of constituent opinion. In the American system there are no Edmund Burkes defiantly asserting that the voters put them in place to exercise their best judgment. Those who get out of touch with opinion back in their states or districts tend to disappear—irrespective of how good their "best judgment" may be.

The decline in authority—of institutions, professions, or established individuals—further reduces the restraint on public opinion. For much of the public celebrity has become as valid a source of judgment as professional knowledge. What Jane Fonda or Robert Redford or Jimmy Swaggart may think carries considerable, perhaps surprising, weight. As for expertise, the tendency today is for interest groups to find and elevate experts based upon agreement with their views. The notion that independent professional judgment should carry weight unhappily has an increasingly far-off sound.

That public opinion grows increasingly powerful provides no guarantee that it will be increasingly wise. Nor does it provide a guarantee that it will be steady. Public opinion can readily be fitful, even shallow, in a democracy. There is no requirement—other than that sense of civic obligation which, regrettably, tends to be steadily less stressed in our society—for public opinion to be serious. A lack of serious, unhappily as well as happily, is the privilege of democracy. The task for true leadership is to limit the play of fitfulness and adequately, if not optimally, to sustain wisdom and steadiness.

This bears on a fourth point that was raised. It is essential in this society for leaders continuously to build toward consensus on substantive issues. American leaders cannot rely on the size of their electoral margins or even the magnitude of electoral landslides. Such triumphs can fade quickly and, in any event, they are normally more of a tribute to the weakness of the political opposition than an indication of the public's willingness to provide a mandate on substance. Nor can leaders today rely, as they could for a quarter century after World War II, on a national consensus—based on the "lessons" of that war and marked by a public willingness to resist both communism and Soviet encroachments. Leaders today must *earn* public support.

The decline of consensus and the return of divisions within the society have been paralled by the reassertion of congressional power. There is little point in mourning that change. Indeed, congressional dominance has been the normal condition for the American democracy throughout much of our history. The principal exception has been during periods of war or international tension, when an external challenge induces congressional deference to the executive. So the leaders of the executive branch should not expect acceptance of their views. Here too they must build support for substantive policies in the Congress.

Let me turn now to some of the consequences that flow from America's unique history and attitudes. It is they that shape our foreign policy. It is they that underlie American exceptionalism, not some special dispensation from the Almighty. The principal consequence is that American foreign policy historically has been based upon "moralism-legalism," the source of despair for practicing diplomats like George Kennan. Certain of the European states have regularly been astonished by the vehement American reaction to, what strike them as, practical steps. To their astonishment that American reaction may occur, not when their move is geopolitically meaningful, but rather when they stray across some legal or moral line that offends American sensibilities.

The Soviets, for example, were astonished, perhaps understandably, by the vehemence of the American response to their movement of troops across the border into Afghanistan in December 1979. After all, the real shift in power and orientation had already occurred some eighteen months earlier, when the Daoud monarchy had been overthrown and a pro-Soviet regime installed. The German government could not anticipate President Wilson's outraged reaction to its decision to embark on unrestricted submarine warfare, which the German High Command regarded as simply a practical necessity. What these nations missed is that American foreign policy is driven, not by concepts of realpolitik or raison d'état, but by the public mood—of revulsion or sympathy. It is the violations of our concepts of legality or of our moral codes that engage the American public—and triggers our response. Contrary to many diplomats (mostly foreign) and scholars impute regarding what American policy must be or should be (that is never clear precisely which), American policy rests very uncomfortably, if at all, on considerations of realpolitik. Such calculations are foreign to the American temperament—and it is the

American temperment that counts. No matter how weighty such considerations, they will either be disregarded or policy will rest upon them only fitfully.

Indeed policy may rest less on realism than upon a foundation that can only be described as romantic. A German friend of mine—to demonstrate that a subtle streak of realpolitik lies beneath the surface of American moralizing—likes to cite an 1814 letter written by Jefferson stating that Bonaparte's domination of the European continent would directly threaten American security:

> Surely none of us wish to see Bonaparte conquer Russia, and lay at his feet the whole continent. This done, England would be but a breakfast . . . put all Europe into his hands and he might spare such a force to be sent in British ships, as I would as leave not have to encounter, when I see how much trouble a handful of British soldiers in Canada have given us. No. It cannot be to our interest that all Europe should be reduced to a single monarchy.

I believe that my German friend misses the essential point. In June 1812, at almost the very moment that Napoleon, having just crossed the Niemen River on his way to the seizure—and subsequent burning—of Moscow, the United States in a wildly romantic gesture threw itself on the side of the very same Bonaparte whose domination of the continent represented so great a threat to the American Republic. The United States had embraced Bonaparte at the very height of his power, just as much of Europe was rallying to his cause, and before his allies and vassals began to desert him *after* the retreat from Moscow.

Indeed, the United States then proceeded to declare war on England, which after Trafalgar was the only nation that could wreak devastation on the United States. England then proceeded to do precisely that, bringing down on our heads far more "trouble" than could a "handful of soldiers in Canada." Why did the United States make this romantic gesture? Largely because we were morally outraged by British impressment of our seamen. Moreover, since those momentous events American decisions have quite regularly been driven less by considerations of national interest than by moral outrage.

I should note in passing that one ought not be beguiled by the notion of realpolitik—the way it is practiced as opposed to the way it is discussed. In Europe policies were less frequently designed by the Bismarcks of this world than by ham-handed and rather doltish imitators, who had learned the words but missed the tune. No greater act of sheer political folly can be imagined than the actions of Ludendorff and the German general staff in 1916 and 1917, while mouthing the precepts of realpolitik, managed to arouse the recumbent and peace-loving United States to deploy its power against

Germany. The sheer folly of the attempts to create a Mexican threat to the United States, culminating in the Zimmermann telegram, or of the decision on unrestricted submarine warfare reflects minds romantically in pursuit of a quixotic "realism." Bismarck must have turned in his grave.

While realpolitik in both practice and logic has sufficient problems not to be burdened with Adolf Hitler, it should be noted that Hitler, a wholly undisciplined romantic who occasionally mouthed the clichés of realpolitik, made a similar and catastrophic blunder. By declaring war on the United States on the day after Pearl Harbor, Hitler solved Roosevelt's political problem. Just as the American people were gearing up to charge across the Pacific to give the Japanese their just desserts, Hitler's declaration of war permitted Roosevelt to direct the preponderance of America's energy to polishing off Germany first.

A second set of consequences flow from America's geographic distance from the centers of great power conflict and America's total regional dominance. This gave to the United States a luxury of choice not available to the other great powers—whether to engage, how to engage, and, indeed, whether to disengage. Only Britain, which could from the fringes of Europe influence the balance of power, had anything in the way of this luxury of choice and, of course, to a much more modest degree. (It should be remembered perhaps, by way of admonition, that England's decisions to engage and then to disengage had given her the unenviable reputation and nickname of "perfidious Albion".)

Since its inception the United States had never, ultimately, been seriously threatened. It does not therefore understand the visceral feeling of nations that have perennially lived with the dread of being conquered. It has thus been free to disregard what for other nations are the practical necessities of the national interest. It can act self-confidently, even blithely. Thus it felt free simply to ignore latent threats distant in time. It has felt free to base its policies on its own moral standards, its own notions of right and wrong.

To be sure the underlying reality has now changed. The development of nuclear weapons and of intercontinental delivery systems has meant that, since the 1960s, the Soviet Union has been capable of severly damaging or, since the 1970s, devastating the United States. In reality we are today dreadfully vulnerable. But that has not meant a transformation of American psychology.

The simple fact that the Soviet Union can, in a few hours time, destroy American life as we have known it implies certain new realities. We can neither disregard nor remove the Soviet Union. In the end we have no choice but to deal with an ideological foe whom we find morally repugnant—not to coin a phrase an "evil empire." But such dealings make many Americans feel uncomfortable and morally tarnished. And from time to time, we may be inclined to say—the devil with any such negotiations.

Another reaction may be simply to reject current reality. If the deepest instinct is to cry out that America has never been and, in the natural order of things, ought not now to be vulnerable then there is a natural quest to restore that rightful condition of American invulnerability. It is this that underlies the popular appeal of the *original* version of President Reagan's Strategic Defense Initiative. It represents a way to restore the American birthright—of invulnerability. It is a way to restore what we alone, among the great powers, have enjoyed.

If we can make nuclear weapons "impotent and obsolete"; if we can shed incoming warheads in the same manner that our roofs shed the rain that falls upon us, then we can once again be invulnerable. Then we need not treat with the evil empires with their morally repugnant ways. We can avoid the moral tarnishing that comes from negotiations or, even worse, from acquiescence in the unacceptable.

It is for the American society an understandable dream, but it is not to be. Even if strategic defenses were to be deployed (and we are a long, long way from that) it would only alter moderately the calculus of nuclear deterrence. As far as the eye can see, throughout the lives of our children and our grandchildren, the Soviet Union will retain the capability to devastate American cities and the American nation. For all the foreseeable future the United States will thus be obliged to rely upon nuclear deterrence to protect itself, It will remain vulnerable. We will be forced to coexist with the Soviets. We will be obliged to negotiate.

There is a third set of consequences that flows from America's psychological inheritance. It is the belief that American policy *must succeed,* if it is morally right— with the companion belief that we will not succeed if we are morally flawed. Indeed that bit of the national creed is fittingly captured in the national anthem:

> For conquer we must,
> When our cause it is just.

Note the conviction that righteousness cannot be denied victory. *There* is American exceptionalism. No continental state, overrun repeatedly over the centuries, could express such a sentiment. Note also that curiously American belief that victory will come if, and only if our cause is just. Given our experience, Americans quite widely believe that, if we fail to be victorious, the cause for which we fight must be immoral. Such views help to explain the difficulty in sustaining public support for counter-insurgencies or "police actions." This was painfully true in Vietnam, and even in Korea, which represented a successful exercise of power, public support visibly faltered.

These sentiments also illuminate the American attitude towards war in general. When it is finally roused to fight, America loves crusades. It loves to smite an evil foe. Victory should be total. The victories over Nazi Germany and Grenada have this, if nothing else, in common.

The use of American arms in a limited way—out of some subtle calculation of the national interest—does not come easily to us. The limited engagement for limited goals will enjoy public support, only if it is also limited in time. What inevitably sets in is disenchantment or, even worse, a conviction that the cause is not just. America, despite its immense strength, is seen to lack staying power. And so we have been reminded by the likes of Pham Van Dong, Hafez el-Assad, and now Daniel Ortega. It is the fear of our allies and dependents; it is the hope of our opponents. All too quickly we become impatient with what is seen as nonsuccess.

The belief that our actions will be crowned with success only if we are engaged in a just cause helps to explain American ambivalence regarding covert operations. For the most part the American people accept the necessity of such operations, but remain uneasy about them. Such actions are legitimate, only if they are carried on, preferably with respectable collaborators, for purposes that are good. By contrast, if we treat with rogues with results seen to be indefensible, no rationale will soothe the public's discontent.

In the wake of the arms scandal and the revelation that we had covertly supplied American arms to the Iranian regime, much, in my view far too much, was said about the supposed parallel with Roosevelt's secret negotiations to provide the British with fifty overage American destroyers in 1940. The parallel was, to say the least, forced. As a justification it was ineffective— and appropriately so. In 1940, no one could be under any illusions regarding Roosevelt's views about the desirability of an Allied victory and the menace of Nazi Germany. Roosevelt's secret negotiations were but an extension of his open diplomacy. There were no contradictions in policy to explain. The cause was just. And we dealt, not with rogues, like Ghorbanifar, but with Churchill and others repected by American people.

By contrast the secret provision of arms to the Ayatollah Khomeini meant under-the-table dealing with a regime the American people understandably loathed. (Mr. Reagan had won the presidency in large measure due to that loathing.) The covert operations represented a *de facto* repudiation of our declared policy. The administration had repeatedly pledged to the American people that we would never negotiate with terrorists. We had tried to persuade our allies and others to refrain from such dealings. We had launched and were continuing Operation Staunch—the attempt to persuade all nations from providing arms to Iran. What we were doing covertly was a flat contradiction of all that we had publicly professed. The public's angry and disgusted reaction to the revelations was no surprise. What was a surprise was that Mr. Reagan had failed (on this one occasion) viscerally to understand where the American people were. In this society covert operations will be accepted only if they are in support of openly declared policy goals.

LET US now consider some important examples of how these basic American attitudes affect the dimensions and effectiveness of American foreign policy. I start with NATO. I hope the reasons are obvious. NATO has been and continues to be the greatest foreign policy success of the United States since the close of World War II—indeed it may be the greatest foreign policy success in American history. But in one sense that success has been easy to achieve. All of the ingredients for effectively engaging the sentiments of the American people are there. Western Europe consists of a set of democratic states; indeed, in Western Europe is the principal array of long-time democracies outside the North American continent. These democracies have visibly been threatened by a heavily militarized, more powerful totalitarian state, the Soviet Union. The American people are linked to Europe by ties of sentiment and (for most of us) by descent. American institutions of government and law are European, primarily English, institutions.

Moreover, twice within this century, the United States has fought—and successfully—to preserve the independence of European nations and extend freedom. No doubt somewhat immodestly, older Americans regard the continued freedom of the nations of Western Europe as a proud, American accomplishment. When the shadow of Soviet power threatened Western Europe in the late 1940s, the United States was prepared to provide what was, in effect, a unilateral guarantee for the defense of Europe. The United States, moreover, proceeded to reconstitute its military forces, and deployed a sizable force in Western Europe where, without precedent, it has been permanently stationed. Despite occasional differences with our allies, the United States has sustained its role, even more than our allies expected. Despite the disenchantment of the Vietnam period and the widespread belief that America should substantially reduce its worldwide role and military deployments, which culminated in the Mansfield Amendment, the United States renewed its commitments to the security of Western Europe and has increased both the number and quality of its forces.

Given their own presuppositions and history, Europeans generally quite misapprehend the nature of the American commitment. The fundmental basis of that tie is sentiment—and the moral engagement of the American people to the security of Europe. Americans by and large see Europeans as good people, worthy democratic peoples, deserving people, threatened in their way of life by a more powerful totalitarian state. Europeans are seen to *deserve* our support. Those sentiments undergird American support for the Alliance. It is not primarily a cold and rational calculation of the national interest.

The Europeans tend to see it differently, particularly the European right. They tend to cast the American commitment in the hackneyed terms of realpolitik. I repeatedly (and with some annoyance) have heard European diplomats and political figures state with apparent certainty: the United States has a national interest in preventing Europe from falling under Soviet domination; since it is in the American national interest, the Americans *must* continue to maintain their forces here and *must continue to provide protection for Europe.* Nothing could be more rational. Nothing could be more wrong. American foreign policy does not rest on such rational calculations.

In its most extreme form this attitude was pungently expressed by Michel Jobert, then French foreign minister, during a rather irritating period in French-American relations in the early 1970s. With Cartesian logic, if not (one hopes) French delicatesse, Jobert used to say: "the Americans have so great an interest in the security of Europe that they cannot leave. . . . You may insult the Americans, you may abuse the Americans, . . . but they must remain . . . their national stake is too great for them to withdraw."

It is a colossal error (perhaps reminiscent of Ludendorff's similar misjudgments) to suggest that the Americans are obliged to stay. It represents a total misunderstanding of the bond that holds the United States in Europe. Why throw Richelieu at an American society that ultimately could care less about raison d'état? Such remarks represent the highest form of European folly. If the American people ever decide that *Europeans are not worth defending*, nothing will hold American forces in Europe or preserve the American commitment—not all the analyses or arguments of diplomats, scholars, or political leaders. Note that I have said "Europeans" worth defending, *not* "Europe" worth defending. It makes clear that American support reflects our ties of sentiments rather than geostrategic considerations.

Of course, I have underscored one European mood, and European moods vary. Indeed, the European mood tends to oscillate between the fear of being dominated by the United States and the fear of being abandoned by the United States. Any change in the status quo tends to stir up the latter fear, as we have observed recently in European discussions of the INF Treaty. Sometimes the very same people, who had previously stated with great firmness that due to its national interest the United States could never leave Europe, will express the fear that withdrawal or reduction of American forces is inevitable.

I shall state my own belief. The United States has maintained the Watch on the Elbe since 1945—for reasons that reflect the American character and values. I would expect that Watch to be maintained so long as it is necessary. It will end only if the threat disappears or, certainly more likely, the Europeans are so foolish as to tear up the ties of sentiment that actually undergird the American commitment. The possibility of that is certainly enhanced, if the Europeans persist in viewing the United States as just another nation, more or less like themselves, whose policies are similarly driven by careful, if ruthless, calculations of the national interest. Indeed, if the United States were really the kind of nation that Europeans portray, our forces in Europe, and our commitment to Europe, would have been substantially reduced years ago.

TO BE sure the American record in foreign policy over the last forty years is rather more mixed than the NATO achievement would suggest. So let us turn from America's greatest foreign policy success to what was her most spectacular failure—and the source of divisions within the country that still plague us. I refer, of course, to Vietnam. Our military involvement in Vietnam extended through the administrations of four presidents. Eisenhower is sometimes added as a fifth, especially by those who idolize Jack Kennedy, and therefore try to blur the reality that it was under their hero that we first became seriously engaged. Ike was too much a military man to believe in gestures, signals, or token forces and involvement. He was also too shrewd to misunderstand the sentiments of his countrymen regarding war. Ike also understood that limited stakes should mean limited involvement.

It is sometimes said that Vietnam was lost because of a lack of public support, and it is then concluded that we must never become involved in any hostilities that the public does not support. As a truism, that may be acceptable. As a guide to policy, it is almost useless. What is forgotten perhaps conveniently, is that at the outset of the war (after the Tonkin Gulf episode in 1964 and the first deployment of ground forces in 1965) there was general, almost universal, support. As the war dragged on without decisive results, disenchantment began to set in. After Tet—effectively, if inaccurately, exploited both by the war's opponents here at home and by the enemy in Southeast Asia—public support sank to low levels and never recovered.

If ever there was the inverse of a Pyrrhic victory, Tet was it. It was a staggering military defeat for the Viet-cong. Indeed, the VC never recovered from it. But given the psychological reaction here, Hanoi might well conclude: another such defeat, we will have won.

What went wrong in Vietnam? The answer is: just about everything. First, there was no *depth* in the support for American involvement. In 1964 and 1965 the American people were prepared to follow their president, just as they had regularly done since Pearl Harbor. But this was more deference to an initial decision than a full commitment to the struggle. Second, by contrast to Western Europe, there were no ties to Vietnam arising from history and sentiment, from common institutions, common experience, and common descent. Third, despite the continuing effort to provide a facade after Diem's overthrow, it was difficult seriously to portray Vietnam as a democracy. Thus, it suffered in terms of legitimacy in the eyes of the American people—a crack in, as it were, the wall of support that could be widened by the war's critics. Indeed, the repeated elections (which always had a somewhat artificial flavor) were designed more to increase the legitimacy of our Vietnam involvement in the eyes of Americans than they were to affect internal development within Vietnam. Perhaps their ultimate purpose was to reassure President Johnson that he was right in leading this crusade.

But, if this were not enough, let me point to grave problems that went beyond the psychological setting.

Fourth, the strategic design of the war was grossly inadequate. It rested ultimately on our persuading Hanoi, i.e., the Lao Dong party, to come to terms. MacArthur may have overstated it a bit when he said: "In war there is no substitute for victory." But one sure as hell ought to have a strategy designed to secure one's political objectives. Since we lacked such a strategy, we were doomed in a sense to a war of attrition. In such a war, while the material resources might be on the side of the United States, quite clearly the psychological resources were in the hands of Hanoi.

The willingness to stake all on the lack of American staying power was stated briefly, and eloquently, indeed prophetically, by none other than Pham Van Dong. In 1965 in a conversation with Bernard Hill, he got it quite simply: "We are going to win, because we are going to make this a long, inconclusive war, and the United States cannot fight long, inconclusive wars."

Fifth, lest my pointing to the flawed political and strategic design of the war suggest that I support the revisionist views now fashionable in American military circles that the loss was all the fault of the politicians, let me hasten to add that the design of military operations was also badly flawed. This is rapidly being forgotten by many who served in Vietnam, and it is certainly not the mythology being learned by junior officers. The military focused on the "war of the big battalions," which it more or less regularly won. It tended to ignore that other and equally crucial "village war," in which the insurgents' control remained largely unchallenged even in the days of massive American deployments. Firepower was applied massively, but unselectively; the sought-after targets remained elusive. The inevitable result was to weaken support *worldwide* for American policy—without attaining any military objectives. In short, an effective military strategy was not undermined by a flawed political strategy. Rather the flawed political strategy was *reinforced* by faulty military strategy.

Sixth, we created the army of Vietnam, the ARVN in our own image. We made it into a capital-intensive force, dependent upon mobility, equipment (and thus spare parts and maintenance), ammunition, fuel. In the end, after the withdrawal we *welshed* (there is no other way to say it) on our commitment to Vietnam and to the forces that we had created in our own image. Congress regularly and repeatedly cut the requested appropriations, ensuring that any problems in the ARVN with personnel would be vastly complicated by problems with matériel. Our failure to live up to our commitment of matériel support makes it possible, if still implausible, for some simply to blame the ultimate defeat in Vietnam on the United States.

I do not share the views of those who felt that the war was doomed from the outset. The conditions were adverse (and this government did not recognize how adverse), but it could have been done. It required one of two things. Either we had to make clear that we were prepared to blow the enemy away and, for whatever reason, this society was not prepared to go this far. (I note that even the Soviets, less constrained either by domestic opinion or world opinion, have been unwilling to go that far in Afghanistan.) Alternatively, we had to demonstrate great insight and skill, neither of which we displayed. Included here was more effectively to inspire, rather than to overshadow, our Vietnamese allies.

This is not the occasion for a lengthy post-mortem on Vietnam. Nor will this be the last post-mortem. What I should like to stress is that the greatest successes of American foreign policy, coming in the first twenty years after World War II, were largely in Europe. This was favorable and familiar terrain, where our power could be matched by knowledge and insight. Our record elsewhere, notably in the third world, is more spotty. There are successes, but there are also failures. Those failures are not really due to a lack of American *power*. Despite the occasional alarms, that is acknowledged worldwide.

The failures flow from lack of knowledge and subtlety. These have rarely been the strong points in American foreign policy—and we have been perhaps insufficently modest in our admission. In the third world we deal with immensely complex conditions, psychologically far distant from the American people. Psychological distance is not bridged by ties of sentiment—in either direction. These are simply the realities. I do not expect to change them. But also I do not think that expectations for American foreign policy should be pitched too high, as if these realities did not exist.

Though I am somewhat reluctant, nonetheless I feel obliged to say a few words on the subject of covert operations. Such operations can be useful, but they should be viewed with prudence rather than with eager anticipation. The "cloak-and-dagger boys" must be restrained or, inevitably, they will get you into trouble. I look therefore with some concern on a set of interlocking covert operations carried on worldwide and with ideological fervor. Such a structure sometimes goes under the label of the Reagan Doctrine. Such operations should not be vast enterprises. Instead they should be low profile, capable of being turned on or off, depending upon an assessment of the potential gains versus costs and risks. In short, a covert operation should not and perhaps can not be a crusade. The prestige of the United States should not be heavily invested in its success or failure. The prestige of the president should not be so invested. When the stakes are raised, the risk of embarrassment grows too large. And one must remember that the appetite for such ventures on the part of the American people is rather limited. If one is to be prudent, one must also be selective. If there is an overload, public support will evaporate.

IT IS time for me to draw some conclusions regarding how well the American style in foreign policy meshes with its responsibilities as a great power. America is a peculiar kind of great power, and other nations come increasingly to recognize that peculiarity, as our preponderance in world affairs diminishes. After World War II America's power was so awesome that its weaknesses could be ignored or quickly forgotten. Today there is great attention to those weaknesses, and consequently, far greater concern.

What is the assessment? America is an unusual kind of great power that had no interest in acquiring its role and responsibilities and from time to time loses interest in them. The United States lacks the cool detachment that a great power should have. For a great power it appears a little soft-hearted, a little too inclined toward feelings of guilt. As a portrait of a nation, it is not altogether bad. But what may be accounted virtues in a nation, may be weaknesses for a great power. The United States, moreover, seems to have a limited sense of history—and what little it has seems to be diminishing. Sometimes it appears that for the American people there is no yesterday and there is no tomorrow, but only the impulses of the moment. We seem foreordained to repeat mistakes that were judged to be such only a few years earlier, because the sense of history and the institutional memory are so limited.

Can the United States sustain the responsibilities that have fallen its way? In the last year the question, Is America in decline? has become something of a fad. In part, this has been stimulated by Paul Kennedy's book, *The Rise and Fall of the Great Powers.* But the interest is driven by more than one scholarly work or even a fad. It is also driven by a concern about the vast federal deficits of recent years and consequently by the immense growth of the national debt. Perhaps even more important, it reflects the deficits in the balance in trade and the balance of payments, the necessity to borrow staggering sums abroad, and the dramatic shift of the United States from the status of great creditor nation to the world's largest debtor.

It is also driven by a belief that our competitiveness has declined, that we are lagging behind other nations in innovation and the growth of productivity. It is also driven by the widely advertised loss of jobs, the decline in the manufacturing base, and the tenaciousness of the trade deficit in the face of a sharp decline in the dollar exchange rate.

All of this is contrasted to the good old postwar days of American dominance. We emerged from World War II with 60 percent of the world's manufacturing capacity, 50 percent of its gross product, etc. Such numbers are contrasted with these of today in which the United States has slipped to roughly 25 percent of the world's output. Moreover, in those earlier days we possessed a monopoly of nuclear weapons and, for a long time thereafter, a substantial preponderance in strategic forces. By contrast, in recent years the president of the United States has repeatedly stated his belief that in every significant catagory of military power the United States is inferior to its principal foe.

For a nation still on top of the world, it is a pretty gloomy prospect. Even given the well-known American proclivity to exaggerate, I believe it is grossly overdone.

The first point to bear in mind is that America's dominant position after the war was an unnatural one. It reflected the substantial destruction in Germany and Japan, the devastation of Europe including European Russia, chaos in China, and the impoverishment of Britain. As production in these countries was restored and grew, our relative position inevitably had to decline. Not only was that position unsustainable, we did all that we could to prevent its being sustained. We bent every effort to helping others rebuild their economies, even though it meant our relative decline. It is scarcely logical, though understandable, to feel nostalgic about an era that we sought so hard to bring to a close. Moreover, if others were to catch up with us in terms of output and living standards, it would be astonishing if we had been able to maintain a technological lead in everything. We have not done so. Perhaps we should have done better, but we have not done all that badly. For a nation with 5 percent of the world's population, 25 percent of the world's output does not seem miserably small.

Similar conclusions seem appropriate with respect to the military balance. It would have been impossible to sustain the military edge that the United States had acquired by the early 1960s. As the Soviet Union built up her strategic forces and acquired a counter-deterrent, the wholly secure position that existed when the United States could devastate any foe without significant fear of retaliation has disappeared. But the United States has immensely impressive military capabilities. In some categories they may be inferior to the Soviets, in other categories they are significantly superior. The North Vietnamese may have been prepared to test America's military capabilities, the Soviets will surely not want to do so.

What we see is a picture of *relative* decline, which was unavoidable given our unnatural and unsustainable position at the close of World War II. That decline has been going on for a long time, though it is just recently that we have been obliged to notice it. That relative decline may, indeed, continue, but it will do so at a much reduced rate.

The United States is no longer economically a preponderant power. It is no longer militarily a dominant power. It can no longer achieve more or less whatever it desires, as it could in the postwar years. Its wishes are no longer fiat around the world. Nonetheless, the United States remains and will long remain the leading world power. Our decline may have been somewhat more rapid than it need be because of our follies—the demobilization of forces after the war, the long Vietnam tragedy, self-indulgence or the lack of discipline in economic matters, particularly in recent years. Nonetheless, the United States is the leading power and will remain so.

In categories other than military its advantages relative to its chief foe, the Soviet Union, remain immense. Even with regard to military power we may have been inclined to exaggerate Soviet strength—in light of the psychological climate of the late 1970s.

The United States will have the economic capacity to provide for its citizens a high and increasing standard of living. Its capacity for innovation remains far more impressive than current wisdom would have it. Its competitiveness is improving. If it does not use it injudiciously, the United States will have the military power to help sustain a reasonably stable world order. The United States may no longer be a Colossus that bestrides the world. Nonetheless, we will remain sufficiently large and powerful that it will be difficult to ignore our wishes. That is really all that we need—and all that we can seriously ask for.

In this light the recent breast-beating, the *Strum und Drang*, the reiterated and exaggerated Sorrows of Young Werther, strike me as grossly exaggerated.

Despite the general decline of authority in America, the authority of Adam Smith has (perhaps surprising) risen of late. In 1777, after the Battle of Saratoga, Adam Smith was hailed in the streets of Edinburgh by an acquaintance: "Dr. Smith, Dr. Smith, have you heard the dreadful news from North America."

"No," responded Smith, "What is it?"

"Burgoyne has been forced to surrender with all his forces. It's the ruination of the country."

"There is a lot of ruin in a nation," responded Smith insightfully if not sympathetically.

We sometimes forget as we watch for those indicators of marginal decline how powerful this nation *is* and how remarkable that power is in relation to virtually all of human history. We will, no doubt err, but those errors will not seriously endanger this Republic. Regrettably those errors may affect other nations—smaller, weaker, and dependent upon us. For that reason we must be particularly careful. As our margin of power declines, we should compensate by striving for greater skill and wisdom. But there is no reason to look to the future with foreboding.

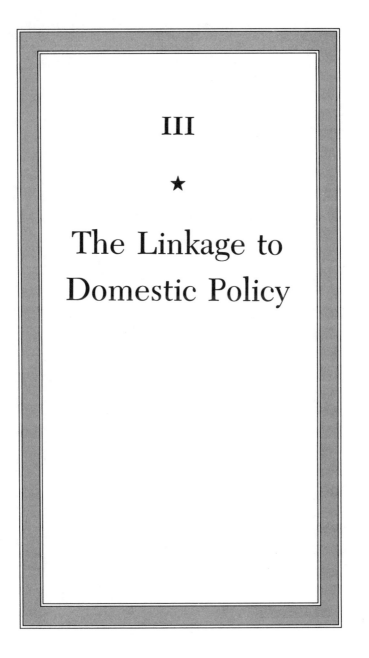

III

★

The Linkage to
Domestic Policy

NDER THE rubric of the special American style in foreign policy, I have presented to you some judgments about foreign policy, and promised that I would conclude by discussing its linkage to domestic policy. In that earlier discussion I pointed to certain unique aspects of the American style in foreign policy. I pointed out that, contrary to what assorted diplomats, generals, intelligence officers, and students of foreign policy may believe or hope, American foreign policy has not been and cannot be based upon those careful calculations of the national interest that pass under the heading of "realpolitik." Instead, the driving force behind American foreign policy must be, in this democracy of democracies, public opinion.

To say public opinion is really to say public passion.

Unless a policy successfully engages the public, it may not be possible to sustain it over the long haul. The public is most likely to remain engaged, if it believes that a policy is morally right. It may also embrace a policy because it is "good for America," but that policy ultimately must survive some moral test. Unless it is sustained by moral conviction, it may not long endure as opinions change or as the costs of the policy increase. It is for this reason that the American people historically have embarked joyously on crusades and have, at best, only tolerated the limited engagement for those reasons of state that might in other societies be more readily embraced.

I have discussed the now-fashionable topic of America's decline. In a sense, my judgment on this subject was somewhat akin to Mark Twain's observation on his reported demise: reports of America's decline are much exaggerated. To be sure, there was no way that the United States could for long maintain the preeminent position in the world with which it emerged at the close of World War II. That elevated condition was based upon transitory factors, most importantly the immense damage that had been inflicted on all the other great industrial nations in the world. Indeed, rather than seeking to preserve its position of material and military advantage, the United States sought to mitigate it by extending material aid to damaged allies, to former enemies, and, subsequently, to nations in the underdeveloped world. We even tried to extend aid to the Soviet

Union and its satellites, but were rebuffed in that quest by Stalin, likely to the regret of his successors in the Kremlin. There is, of course, a flat contradiction between helping to build up others and attempting to preserve a position of extraordinary pre-eminence. Contrary to the unconscious, if ambivalent, desires of the American society, there is no way simultaneously to move toward both goals. Yet, as our moods swing, we sometimes mourn those lost days of immense American material advantage. It is then that we may grow giddy with talk of American decline.

To be sure, that relative decline, some of which was both desirable and unavoidable, has in the last quarter century gone further than we might have liked, reflecting a kind of indifference on our part—a lack of diligence and a lack of discipline. Others have been more vigorous and more industrious than we have been— their growth rates in investment and innovation more impressive than our own. American goods have, to a large extent, lost the reputation for quality, and also, for a time, appeared overpriced in relation to those of others. As the American trade deficit grew, and particularly the deficit in the manufacturing account, we began to regale ourselves with stories vividly demonstrating how uncompetitive the United States had become. Some of that was true. More of it was exaggerated. And, as far as the price aspect is concerned, it remained heavily dependent upon the gross overvaluation of the U.S. dollar which has subsequently (and inevitably) disappeared.

I concluded on a somewhat reassuring note that the alarmists and crepe-hangers among us may find difficult to accept. The United States remains the world's largest and, in most respects, most powerful economy and will remain so for the foreseeable future. For better or worse, the rest of the world cannot afford to ignore either the American economy or American policy. What is more, we are now on the verge of the restoration of the American manufacturing base. In addition, the United States possesses the most sophisticated and, for most military objectives, the strongest military establishment in the world. Our period of dominance may be over (partly through our own action and volition). Yet, for the foreseeable future, the United States will continue to possess the world's leading economy, will remain an indispensable counterweight to Soviet military power, and will continue to play the leading role in preserving international stability.

We should not allow appropriate concern about our competitive performance to cross the line to self-detraction. We should, of course, strive to solve our problems, to become more competitive, to restore discipline and innovation, and the like. Nonetheless, we should not fall prey to that old American habit of extrapolating past trends, pointing to some hypothetical future outcome, and then imposing that hypothetical future on the present.

Let us do better, but let us not berate ourselves in the interim. Let us free ourselves from our present dependency in balancing the national economic accounts on an immense annual importation of foreign capital. To do so, we shall probably have to solve the problem of the federal deficit but these things do not suggest a near-term termination of America's international role. We are far more resilient then that would suggest. As Adam Smith once stated: "there is a lot of ruin in a nation."

While the U.S. economy is not nearly as vigorous as that of Japan or of the four Asian tigers, and while it diverts a large share of national output to defense (while devoting a disproportionate share of domestically generated savings to financing the deficit), still it is doing quite well vis-à-vis its main rival, the Soviet Union. Moreover, a combination of its overall size, the size of its domestic market, and its role as international banker will continue to provide it with the leading position on international economic matters. Despite the hype and journalistic hoopla, it is still too early to hang out the crepe.

One can say, whether by way of condemnation or of mere observation, that the condition of the federal budget and the international economic position of the United States have become the playthings of domestic politics. One can think of that as a condemnation, a homily, or an inducement to better performance. But, really, it is simply a statement of fact, fairly close to a truism. But what is true for these specific matters is also true for foreign policy. Given the primacy of public opinion, foreign policy is the "plaything" or, more precisely, the product of domestic politics. In any democracy, foreign policy is domestic politics. That is peculiarly the case in the American Democracy.

A whole collection of professionals and pundits may find this an offense. I refer to those whom I have repeatedly rounded up as the usual suspects—the diplomats, generals, and students of foreign policy. Since America's coming of age, such professionals have regularly admonished us to accept *the primacy of foreign policy.* Indeed, during the period of American dominance—and of American consensus—their views were reasonably if superficially effective in persuading the society of that primacy, usually under the rubric "politics stops at the water's edge." With the breakdown of the foreign policy consensus, it has become evident that the roots of the belief in the primacy of foreign policy are rather shallow. Indeed, the primacy of foreign policy is but a simple translation from the German, *das Primat der Aussenpolitik,* which a generation of European proselytizers of realpolitik have sought to impose upon this exuberant democracy. It does not take. In two out of three encounters, when there is a conflict, domestic politics will win hands down.

So, if we are realistic, we will acknowledge that here foreign policy is domestic politics. We may deflect but we will not dissolve the various interest groups that seek to influence American policy. To take the most prominent example: so long as Israel retains its impressive hold on American public opinion, no political party and few presidents will be prepared to press Israel hard. Turkey will remain under scrutiny, if not under pressure, so long as the Greek-American community has its way. Policies toward Eastern Europe will be strongly influenced by the Polish-American community, as well as by more recent groups of immigrants. Example can be piled on example. It may be the glory of the pluralist society, but it is the source of unending frustration for Foreign Service officers. Theodore Roosevelt unburdened himself of some choice comments on hyphenated Americans, which had a greater persuasiveness when the American ideal was the melting pot, than it does today when that ideal has been modified into ethnic diversity.

Lobbies, of course, can be ideological as well as ethnic. The so-called China lobby, in combination with the heavy-handed policies of the new Chinese regime, serve to frustrate American diplomacy toward the People's Republic of China for some twenty years after the Korean War.

Let us not pursue a wholly elusive dream. Let us accept that foreign policy *is domestic politics*. That obliges us to accept at least some of the implications. One of those realities reflects the constraints imposed upon a president by the constituencies he finds it hard to reach. But these also represent opportunities for presidents with other constituencies. It required a Nixon to overcome the resistance and to achieve a diplomatic breakthrough to China. As recent events have demonstrated, a Ronald Reagan can provide a legitimacy to arms control measures that Jimmy Carter could not. By contrast, a Democratic president, if he desires to do so, could with public support bash the Sandinistas in a manner that will always be denied to Ronald Reagan. In brief, Republican presidents can seek openings to the Communist world without provoking vehement opposition. Democratic presidents, who might be more eager to do so, would be suspect for precisely the same moves. Yet, perhaps ironically, Democrats are free to whack the Communists without initially generating much controversy. It was that policy leeway that lured President Johnson into Vietnam, an involvement that a Dwight Eisenhower could readily avoid.

Such is the asymmetry that varied domestic constituencies may impose upon foreign policy, Or, if you will, the unfairness imposed upon different presidents —for, in an abstract sense, it is rather unfair. I do not want to thrust upon you the conclusion that, if you want to achieve a controversial foreign policy goal, vote for a president from the party opposed to that policy. That would, no doubt, be too paradoxical. Nonetheless, there is a kernel of truth in the observation.

In American foreign policy there are the symmetries as well as the asymmetries. There is no controversy over aid to the Afghan rebels; the two parties compete to aid the Mujahadeen. Politicians of both parties vie with each other to support Israel and to impose sanctions on South Africa. No political party advocates building bridges to the Ayatollah Khomeini. There is little public support for either a long-term "strategic relationship" with Iran or even a dialogue, as the administration has recently, if painfully, discovered. No party advocates abandoning Western Europe to the Soviets. In some ways those symmetries are more interesting than the asymmetries. They point to areas of surviving consensus in the public mind. Presidents, if they are wise, will treat such areas as no-no's, and approach them with extraordinary caution.

If foreign policy is domestic politics, we are obliged to examine politics in all its exuberance. It is a fascinating, if somewhat grubby, subject. The competition for power inevitably is one in which restraint yields to temptation. The glory of democracy is that we resolve the issues of power in a relatively peaceful, if not entirely ethical, manner. Heads are not broken; blood is not shed; there are not the expulsions or deliberate assassinations, or seizures of power that mark other systems. One ought not underestimate such benefits.

But politics inevitably will remain an offense to the philosophers and the moralists. Politics is colorful, disorderly, and disordered. Indeed politics is a kind of syllabus of errors in logic: *non-sequiturs, post hoc ergo propter hoc's*, improper associations, including guilt by association. For the philosophers and moralists there is a kind of absurdity to politics. Political philosophy may seek to extract principles for appropriate political behavior. But politics resists abstractions.

Politics is painfully, almost prosaically, concrete. Tip O'Neill may have overstated the matter, when he remarked that "all politics is local," nonetheless, one is ill-advised to assume that purely national advantages, let alone universal principles are sufficient to generate support on a issue. To academics the fact that a congressional committee chairman comes from some specific state or district may be purely adventitious, if not irrelevant. If one is attempting to move legislation through the Congress, one had best not blithely disregard such simple realities.

But the game of politics must also be played at the wholesale or national level. One must galvanize the voters, if one is to obtain majorities to be elected or to gather support for policies after one is elected. And politics in the large has been undergoing substantial change during recent decades. To be sure, praising one's own wares and undermining one's opponents have always been just the normal stock-in-trade in elections. But these perennial ingredients of electoral politics have undergone almost a transformation since the advent of television, and, one might say, have in a sense been "perfected." There has been a veritable explosion of advertising—and of campaign costs. Since TV provides only the impression of an instant, ingenuity focuses on the image that can be conveyed in a moment. Television both exploits and reinforces the electorate's short attention span. While the public may ultimately grow skeptical (as it has regarding commercial advertising), for the moment such techniques seem to work.

I would be the first to concede that elections have *never* depended upon a serious examination of the issues. Elections also contain a high component of entertainment. No doubt, the public expects to be entertained. Any politician who fails to do so is likely to have a difficult road in politics. That has been true, probably from the beginning, but clearly so in recent decades for the Robert Tafts, Richard Nixons, and Michael Dukakises of this world. The most effective politicians —the Franklin Roosevelts, the Ronald Reagans—understand this full well. The danger comes only if entertainment becomes a substitute for the substance of government.

While politics has always featured entertainment, the carnival aspect of politics seems to have grown in recent years. A public willingness to accept, if only temporarily, magic solutions to problems, so long as they have been sufficiently hyped-up, has expanded the confidence game aspect of politics.

Programs are sold in the same way as candidates. Slogans make things simple. And we have always had slogans—"Remember the Maine," "A war to end war," "The Four Freedoms." But in recent years the exaggerated hype embodied in such slogans has been downgraded from mobilizing the public for war to engaging

(81)

the public in much more mundane issues, such as welfare programs, tax policies, weapons systems, etc. Some of you can still recall the astonishing hoopla associated with the Peace Corps during the Kennedy years. You will recall even more vividly the wilder expectations embodied in President Johnson's War on Poverty. Can one recollect the miracles that Head Start was destined to achieve? And President Reagan's Strategic Defense Initiative is much the same thing. Though it remains, at best, a collection of hopes and technical experiments, it has been treated as if it provided us with an end to the nuclear threat or at least the ballistic missile threat. It is, or course, the grandest entertainment. The TV networks can present the animations or animated cartoons (which they mislabel "news") showing laser beams zapping Soviet missiles during the boost phase. For the moment, that all remains the gleam in the eyes of some technologists—a combination of Buck Rogers and P. T. Barnum.

I have already mentioned Santayana's observation that America is a vast prairie swept by one universal bonfire. It helps to explain these political fads that come to dominate American life. Television, of course, plays its indispensable role in focusing the public's attention on them. I have just listed a few of the more suspect peacetime examples from the War on Poverty to the SDI. But what we may fail to understand is that these proclivities have overtaken even so mundane a matter as budgetary policy. We all recall the tax revolt of the 1970s, California's

Proposition 13 and the like. Associated with this was a curious intellectual phenomenon called supply-side economics. It wasn't economics; it was alchemy. It suggested that by reducing tax rates, we had an automatic formula for increasing revenues. If we cut tax rates, so much more economic activity would result that the revenues lost through the fall in tax rates would be more than replaced in tax collections. It provided a kind of gusher of revenues. It was a budgetary version of the Indian rope trick.

Well, the bonfire, as Santayana would have had it, of supply-side economics swept over the United States in 1981. Many of the respected organs of public opinion, such as the *Washington Post*, urged that we give these new ideas a chance. Being open-minded about new ideas is, of course, a good thing. Regrettably many of the new ideas turn out to be simply bad old ideas dressed up as new ideas. When, in 1981, I argued that President Reagan's tax cuts ultimately doomed his intended defense built-up, and described the recent Tax Act as "the single most irresponsible fiscal action of modern times," I was regarded as something of a spoilsport.

In the good old days one could count upon the Republican party to be the part of fiscal responsibility. Regrettably that is no longer the case. The Republicans turn out to be no more interested in avoiding deficits than the Democrats. . . . so long as the deficits are incurred in a proper cause. Once the GOP learned that deficit financing could be used for so productive and satisfying a purpose as to cut tax rates, particularly for the "deserving rich," the inhibition against deficit financing seemed to have gone away, just as it had for the Democrats, when they found that deficit financing would permit a whole set of domestic programs, also presumably deserving. Indeed, the magnitude of the deficits in recent years have actually shocked the Democrats into a sense of fiscal responsibility—more out of a belief that such vast deficits actually endangered domestic programs than out of a sense that fiscal responsibility is desirable for itself. Among Republicans, to recall the cherished values of bygone days is to be old-fashioned, a "fiscal conservative" (now an expression of mild disparagement): it shows one is just not with it. Such views identify one with the so-called root-canal wing of the Republican party—to which, I must confess, I belong.

In any event, we have now reached a kind of fiscal dead center. The public is quite wary of any tax increases, especially income taxes, so-called "revenue enhancement" can go only so far. Social Security remains unassailable, and the rest of the domestic budget has been squeezed about as much as politically tolerable. Interest payments will, of course, continue to rise, reflecting the growing national debt. Deductions can come only from what can be chiseled out of the defense budget, a possibility which is fostered by the new climate of detente. So the deficit is likely to continue. With the domestic savings rate as low as it is, we shall only gradually free ourselves from the dependency on importing foreign capital.

Domestic policy to a large extent involves the allocation of resources. Subject to our own actions and partly through fate a condition has been created in which it is immensely difficult for us to think much about adjusting allocations through federal policy. What that means is government policy regarding resource allocation is frozen. Some people may think it is a good thing. It certainly has its favorable aspects if one is hoping to avoid creation or deflect augmentation of frivolous programs. But it also tends to preclude quite sensible adjustments. Even those who have welcomed these deficits as a way of heading off new domestic programs may recognize those drawbacks—when their own oxen are being gored.

The largest *ox* is the defense program. (I continue with the earlier oxen metaphor, but I would not want you to draw any further conclusions from it.) The Reagan defense build-up, which was intended in the 1981 budget revisions to rise to almost 9 percent of the Gross National Product, has been terminated, indeed reversed. Defense spending is topping out at about $300 billion a year, perhaps $60 to $75 billion a year more than would have been the case if the earlier tendencies under the Carter program had been carried through. Budget authority for defense is approaching $200 billion a year *less* than it was planned to be at this stage. The share of the GNP going to defense is dropping back toward the 6 percent mark and, no doubt, will fall below it.

What is most interesting about the collapse of the defense build-up is that it has had scarcely any impact on political rhetoric—which continues more or less as if the build-up were proceeding. The press continues to describe "the greatest peacetime military build-up in history," even though there has been scarcely any growth of the force structure. In terms of the force balances the Soviets continue to outnumber us more or less to the same extent that they did in 1981. According to the logic espoused by the president, the United States remains inferior to the Soviet Union in almost all important weapons catagories. Meanwhile the critics of defense expenditures (whom nothing will ever satisfy) continue to refer to "the immense defense build-up" and continue to argue that defense expenditures should not be "sacrosanct," as if real defense expenditures and military manpower were not shrinking.

The allocation for defense, because it is so immense, is also driven by public opinion. At the end of the 1970s and in the early 1980s, the public, frightened by Soviet gains and Soviet attitudes, demanded a strengthening of defense. By the middle 1980s the public, persuaded that America was again "standing tall," that defense expenditures were wasteful, and recognizing that defense was squeezing some popular domestic programs, ceased to support higher defense expenditures, and the expansion came to an end. Whenever any prominent and responsible group comments on defense expenditures, it urges that these expenditures be stabilized, so that the Department of Defense can effectively plan ahead.

That such stabilization is desirable, from the defense standpoint, goes without saying. That it is achievable in practice is a far more dubious proposition. Given the size of defense expenditures, given its status as the chief component of discretionary spending, given the swings in the public mood regarding the wastefulness of defense spending, given real changes in the international environment, it is only prudent that we not expect too much in the way of stabilization of defense spending. It is more or less inevitable that defense spending undergo substantial fluctuations, though not necessarily fluctuations as large as those of recent years. Dependency upon continued public support implies that, whenever that public support lags, there are just too many other things to be done with those pots of money. Commissions, no doubt, will continue to extol the virtues of stabilizing defense expenditures, the Department of Defense would not be wise to presuppose that such stabilization will come anytime soon.

All this points to why defense is never going to be marked by so high a level of efficiency that journalists will find little to write about under the heading of waste. It is impossible to achieve efficiency when resources undergo such wide fluctuations. Just as one has expanded production lines, one is forced to curtail production to uneconomic levels in order to live within new budget limits. Given such fluctuations, and given other government policies, the defense industry finds little incentive to invest its capital in cost-reducing plant and equipment. And the government itself, the financial source of much of the plant and equipment created, has little incentive to devote the resources to achieving significantly lower costs.

These difficulties do not justify failing to do as well as one can under these circumstances. There are degrees of inefficiency in the use of defense resources. Regrettably, there is some tendency for the public (and for others including high government officials) to confuse defense spending with defense posture. They are not synonymous. There must be a defense strategy—more than getting the top dollar. Strategy is the means best to employ resources to obtain political-military ends. A strategic vision should, more or less, govern the various components of defense expenditure. Failure to have such a strategic design for defense not only wastes resources but must ultimately undermine public support for defense. And finally, one should recognize that the flush years will come to an end. One should not enter into mortgages in the fat years that will lead to imbalanced forces later on when the lean years come, as they inevitably will.

I stress these forces affecting the defense budget because it is a primary element in how domestic policy affects our international position. The perception of

American power determines our ability to get things done internationally, the ease or difficulty of dealing with both friend and foe. A substantial weakening of our military posture will mean an undermining of *deterrence in its broadest sense* and may encourage others to run risks that they would not embrace, if they felt the United States to be both powerful and watching. If this be the case, the resources invested to repair the consequences of failed deterrence are likely to be vastly greater than the savings obtained from the slimming down of our defense posture.

SWINGS IN public support for defense expenditures both reflect and reinforce swings in the public mood regarding foreign affairs generally. I earlier stressed some of the unique elements, if not the ironies, in America's role as a dominant world power. It is a great power with a varying attitude toward the power game and a disregard for the usual calculations of realpolitik. From time to time it becomes rather inattentive toward its role and responsibilities. Briefly put, it lacks the steadiness that normally has been associated with great powers in the pursuit of their objectives. That is, from a policy standpoint, a dreadful lack. Inevitably it undermines the continuity of our foreign policy. It causes great nervousness among our allies and dependents.

It is something that we should strive to mitigate, if not to cure. Some degree of continuity is required, if we are to fulfill our international role. We should strive to do better. Given the nature of the American society and the dependency of foreign policy on public opinion, we are unlikely to come any where near perfection. Other nations, those that depend upon us, will have to accept this variability, like it or not. As former Chancellor Helmut Schmidt once put it: I cannot change the Americans, I shall have to make do with them, as they are.

The variability to which I have just referred, which results in wide swings in public attention, is even more evident in domestic policy than in foreign policy. It is perhaps better that way, because foreign policy requires some degree of continuity. Although such continuity may be desirable, it is not essential in domestic policy. The principal cost of such variability is economic, and this after all, is rich in society. In the changes that affect domestic policy we can see the marks of Santayana's universal bonfire. The tides of fashion come and go— and then are forgotten.

If we look back over the last three decades we can see vast such tides. After the domestic alarm that occurred in 1957 with the flight of the Soviet *Sputnik,* there was a cry for improved quality and discipline in education. There was funding; there was a call for scientific training and literacy; there was the New Math (an experiment which proved wholly abortive). After John Kennedy took office there was a steady focus on the space program, destined ultimately to put Americans on the moon. Later in the 1960s there was President Johnson's War on Poverty, which held public attention for a brief period—until it was wiped out by the discontents over Vietnam. In the 1970s there were the various alarms embodied in the energy crisis. For an extended period close attention was paid to energy issues; in the 1980s that attention has virtually disappeared.

That powerful new medium of television, which I discussed earlier, has the ability to focus attention and rapidly to shift attention to some new area. Before television, ideas tended to have greater staying power. What TV has done is to contribute to the shortening of the attention span. In turn, the short-attention span has contributed to the rise of political bunkum. If political bunkum generates support, but is also quickly forgotten so that one pays no penalty for its use, political bunkum is likely to increase.

The short attention span permits an almost instantaneous change of substantive position. I mentioned earlier the curious phenomenon of supply-side economics. Its original justification was that it would generate a higher savings rate and would lead to higher investment, higher productivity, and increased economic activity. Moreover, the increase in economic activity would supposedly generate additional revenues that would more than offset the revenue loss coming from the reduced tax rates. The logic was circular, and should have been unconvincing. When the tax rate reductions were actually implemented, there was actually a decline in the savings rate and no noticeable rise in productivity. We can see from the immense federal deficits that the hope that the revenue loss coming from lower tax rates would be more than offset by increased revenues from greater economic activity and more rapid growth has proved fallacious. What we then saw was a sudden change in a substantive position. The original justification for the supply-side tax cuts was abandoned, and the policies were justified on the basis that they had provided an economic stimulus—not on the supply side but on the demand side. In short, the justification for the tax cuts was, without any acknowledgement, transmuted into a form of Keynesianism.

Some light is shed on such phenomena by a recent study that may provide an important contribution to the understanding of American politics. I refer to an erudite and penetrating article, written by the chairman of the Philosophy Department at Yale University, Dr. Harry Frankfurt. It is entitled "Reflections on Bullshit." I cite it to demonstrate that, though I am no longer an academic, I have a high regard for first-rate academic work. Needless to say, I commend it to all of you—for its substance rather than for its choice of words. You should also understand that the key word in the title is used only in its technical sense.

I cite Professor Frankfurt at some length—even though it requires me to use the B-word.

Bullshitting involves a kind of bluff. It is closer to bluffing, surely, than to telling a lie. . . . Just what is the relevant difference between a bluff and a lie?

Lying and bluffing are both modes of misrepresentation or deception. Now, the concept most central to the distinctive nature of a lie is that of falsity: the liar is essentially someone who deliberately promulgates a falsehood. Bluffing too is typically devoted to conveying something false. Unlike plain lying, however, it is more especially a matter not of falsity but of fakery. This is what accounts for its nearness to bullshit. For the essence of bullshit is not that it is false but that it is phony.

Professor Frankfurt then goes on to cite a father's advice to his son: "Never tell a lie when you can bullshit your way through."

Few in politics need to have that lesson. An art in politics is to sidestep the truth. Regrettably, there are signs that that tendency is on the increase. While Professor Frankfurt indicates that he will "not consider the rhetorical uses and misuses of bullshit"—which, no doubt, demonstrates that his interest lies in philosophy rather than in political science—I shall provide a few examples. I will place such examples under a category that I shall more delicately label bunkum.

In the past, political bunkum has reached a peak during election runs, but then has mercifully fallen away as the normal processes of government take over. Regrettably, the cyclical remission from bunkum has lessened in recent years. In the past, the federal budget has been an authoritative document. It might put the most favorable face possible on certain components of revenue or expenditure, but in the large it has been regarded as a truthful and therefore relevant document. In recent years, regrettably, the truth has been stretched to the point that the federal budget can only be described as phony, to use Dr. Frankfurt's word. I only need cite the contrast between projections of the deficit and the ultimate results. A former director of the OMB, David Stockman, came out from behind the wall of bunkum one day to state: we face $200 billion a year deficits as far as the eye can see. The happy part of the story is that there has been an alternative. As the credibility of the budget projections of the executive branch have declined, the Congressional Budget Office has been turned to for judgments which are looked upon as honest and authoritative. It is a happy indication that the truth will out.

Let me turn now to another area in which I have had some experience—energy. When I joined the Atomic Energy Commission in 1971, I soon learned that there was a eagerly held and rather angry view that "there were three kinds of lies—lies, damn lies, and energy lies." At the time, much of that distrust was coming to focus on nuclear power. It seemed to me that one of the explanations was that the public did not have access to the regulatory arm of the AEC, which operated in a classified area behind security walls. One had to have either a Q-clearance or special permission to be admitted. Secrecy of that sort inevitably breeds distrust—public distrust. I ordered that the facility be released from security requirements so that the public would have access. I cite this only as an illustration of how suspicions tend to be fostered.

I think it fair to say that since 1973 serious observers have acknowledged that the United States has an energy problem. The United States has the largest appetite for oil in the world—5 percent of the world's population represents about one-third of total free-world oil consumption. Our domestic resources are being depleted. In the lower 48 states production has fallen by more than 40 percent since the peak in the early 1970s. It will continue to fall. The disproportion between America's appetite for oil and its capacity to produce would seem to be a simple fact. It implies that inevitably the United States will become more dependent upon foreign sources of supply. It should also be clear that it would be prudent for the United States, in view of its international responsibilities, to avoid becoming excessively dependent upon sources of supply in the world's most volatile region—the Persian Gulf. Therein lies the heart of our energy problem, and that is what energy policy should focus on.

In fact, this country has vast difficulty in so focusing. For the general public an "energy crisis" has nothing to do with the international responsibilities of the United States. An energy crisis for the public occurs when the price of gasoline and other products rises. If the price of gasoline is falling, irrespective of geostrategic considerations, public concern lapses. One consequence is that the United States oscillates in its view of energy matters between complacency and panic. (Need I add we are now in a period of complacency?)

Low oil prices are not only politically soothing, they provide a macroeconomic stimulus and ease the problems of inflation, high interest rates and the like. But low oil prices are seductive, for they imply a more rapidly growing national security problem through a negative impact on domestic oil production and growing dependency on foreign and insecure sources of supply. By contrast, high oil prices, while economically punishing, tend to alert us to the longer-term energy problem. They also provide a stimulus to domestic oil production and slow down the growth of dependency on foreign sources of supply. At the moment the energy position of the United States is becoming increasingly more vulnerable. Domestic production continues to fall. Our appetite for oil is growing once again. Imports have increased by 50 percent in the last two years, and by the mid-1990s the United States will be importing more than 10 million barrels of oil a day, if it should be available, much of it from the volatile Middle East.

As a nation, we have considerable difficulty facing up

to these realities. In periods of complacency it is almost impossible to develop a serious energy policy, and in periods of panic we try to do things that are counterproductive. Formulating energy policy in the United States is extraordinarily difficult. The public's principal desire is to have low energy prices, but that may not reflect economic reality, certainly not long term reality. Energy issues tend to pit region against region, industry against industry, producers against consumers and, if I may say so, economic class against economic class. It makes formation of a consensus on energy policy (as opposed, say, to foreign policy) a difficult and uphill task.

To this, politicians respond by pretending that there is no problem. When he was a candidate in 1980, for example, Mr. Reagan reassured us by stating that "there is more oil in Alaska than there is in Saudi Arabia." (On that observation, he should receive a grade of 5 percent.) Mr. Reagan was thus suggesting that the United States would have no problem with oil supply, if only the government (which was the problem and not the solution) would only get out of the way. As president, Mr. Reagan has subsequently felt obliged to send the Navy to the Persian Gulf, and his justification is to avoid the renewal of gasoline lines. The view that the supposedly immense resources of Alaska could satisfy America's appetite for oil has apparently gone away. Nonetheless, we are now in a period of complacency and, consequently, we are simply not facing up to our energy problems. We are today sowing the seeds of the next energy crisis, likely to come in the mid-1990s.

As an old energy official—indeed one whom the press called "a czar"—I must state categorically that America's performance on nuclear power is nothing short of a disgrace. While Japan and France, using American-developed technologies, proceed to provide themselves with low-cost nuclear power, avoiding the use of oil and the potentially deleterious effects of burning too much coal, the United States has made a total mess of its program. No American utility today will order a nuclear plant. It it were to do so, its board of directors would appropriately face stockholder suits. We have in America provided a tangle of laws that makes efficient construction and operation of plants immensely difficult, and in some cases impossible. That tangle of laws has created an opportunity for guerrilla warfare, which the opponents of nuclear power have been quick to exploit.

At this time the State of New York has been blocking the operation of a nuclear power plant on Long Island, quite at variance with the intention of the Atomic Energy Act, which established the supremacy of federal authority in this area. The consequence is that the costs of this idle plant are increasing at roughly $50 million a month, which somebody will have to pay for. That somebody is likely to include the taxpayers of New York. In order to disguise the impact of its actions, the state is providing the reassurance that rate payers on Long Island will pay less for their electric power if a $5 billion plant is not permitted to operate than if it is. This demonstrates, I believe, that bunkum is not confined to the federal government.

I should emphasize that the problems of nuclear power in the United States are not attributable exclusively to the regulatory disgrace. The intent of the 1954 amendments to the Atomic Energy Act was to allow almost any utility, large or small, qualified or unqualified, to build a nuclear plant. The result has been that the utility industry has performed poorly overall in plant construction. Those problems of course have been immensely intensified by the regulatory morass. But the structure of the utility industry in the United States, reflecting in part the Public Utility Act of 1935, has made it difficult for this country best to exploit this demanding new technology in the way that, for example, France and Japan have exploited it. Finally, one should not neglect the contributory role of labor unions, architects-engineers, and nuclear plant vendors. Though the chief responsibility lies with the legal framework and the regulatory framework, almost all parties have made their contribution to what has become a uniquely American disaster.

I HAVE spent some time on the energy problem, because it is an area in which the failure to resolve fundamental differences regarding national objectives has created a special problem. The American system of governance, so demanding of consensus and so lacking in discipline, is particularly vulnerable in matters such as the energy problem. The American people demand to be well supplied with energy, but there is always some group ready to fight the siting of a power plant in the neighborhood. We want domestic energy supply, but we are reluctant to allow the exploration and development activities that are necessary—or even the pipelines or transmission lines that are required to bring the energy to us. Not only have we failed to solve problems of energy versus the environment, for the most part we have failed to acknowledge the fundamental questions. The result is that the country will suffer from costs that are higher and supplies that are more erratic than they should be. Inevitably there will be a day of reckoning.

I have stressed the energy problem, in part because I am familiar with it, painfully familiar. But the remarks that I have made about energy might be focused in other areas with almost equivalent force. It reflects an unwillingness to face up to problems or an inability to solve them. I could have discussed agricultural policy. I could have discussed the prospective costs of retirement in a society in which the population is aging. (When one speaks of special interests one should recognize that the elderly are the best organized and most effective interest group in the country.) I could have discussed the administration's program to provide a deficit-free budget or "a world free of nuclear weapons." I want only to underscore the point that the American system not only tolerates a high degree of inefficiency in formulation and executing domestic programs, but such inefficiencies are built into the system.

For reasons that I shall come to in a moment I do not regard this, although costly, as catastrophic. In fact, as I shall come to, I see certain benefits in these arrangements. I remind you of the wisdom of Adam Smith—of the capacity of the society to tolerate inefficiency and error. "There is," as he observed in expressing his skepticism about the doomsayers, "a lot of ruin in this country." We must recognize that political incoherence is in a sense the price of freedom. Conflict and internal divisions are a reflection of that freedom. Inefficiencies in government go with its counterpart, the "relatively" efficient performance of the private-sector economy. Government is that area in which we fight out our differences. Therefore, delays and difficulties are to be expected, indeed, in a sense, welcomed.

This is a rich society, and therefore provides a great deal of latitude for inefficiency as a way of preserving our freedoms. Of course, freedom must be defended externally as well as internally. We have had a notable external threat in the Soviet Union. From time to time we have been greatly, perhaps excessively, concerned about that threat. But we need not achieve some optimal level of efficiency in order to preserve our freedom. All we need to do is do better than the Soviet Union, which is a model of economic and bureaucratic inefficiencies. In a sense, what our regulatory apparatus has done to nuclear power, the Soviet regime has done to the entire Soviet economy.

I do not want to be unduly reassuring. On foreign policy it is essential that we take the longer view, that we look adequately to the future. I believe that the United States has done that since the 1930s and *I hope* that we will continue to do so. The counterpart of that observation is that on domestic policy it is far more difficult to take the long view. It is subject to all of the impediments of changing public opinion, of reassuring political bunkum that disguises the problems, and of the difficulty to generate sufficiently intense public reaction to deal with a problem long term. But for reasons I have indicated, one should not despair. One of the benefits of freedom is the privilege to be somewhat sloppy in terms of one's domestic performance.

I have referred repeatedly to this nation as a democracy of democracies. Need I say again that democracy provides, not necessarily for efficient government, but for freedom. That freedom is in itself a product of rather special historical forces, which we should value. Our freedom has been bequeathed to us not only by the special peoples who settled this country, but by those extraordinarily far-sighted individuals whom we call the Founding Fathers, and whose performance in creating the Constitution we celebrated last year. I have mentioned the role that the Puritan inheritance has played in forming this nation's psyche. We should remember that this is a nation that has been formed by various groups of dissidents, including those that lack that official designation. So I conclude with these words from that distinguished Puritan figure, John Milton, who stated in his *Areopagitica*, what I believe must continue to be the ultimate faith of this society: "And though all the winds of doctrine were let loose to play upon the earth, so Truth be in the field, we do injuriously. . . . to misdoubt her strength. Let her and Falsehood grapple: whoever knew Truth put to the worse, in a free and open encounter?"

That is the creed of a free society—of our society. It represents a faith that through conflict ultimately truth will emerge. That is the appropriate way for society to resolve its differences, rather than attempting to sweep away such issues through official dogma. Milton goes on to say: "For who knows not that Truth is strong, next to the Almighty?"

We are prepared as a society to accept the vicissitudes of public opinion, the inefficiencies, the errors of the short term because we believe that through freedom the most rewarding and the most valid policies will more reliably emerge in the long term.

INDEX

★